ISBN 978-0-483-22752-1
PIBN 10186471

This book is a reproduction of an important historical work. Forgotten Books uses state-of-the-art technology to digitally reconstruct the work, preserving the original format whilst repairing imperfections present in the aged copy. In rare cases, an imperfection in the original, such as a blemish or missing page, may be replicated in our edition. We do, however, repair the vast majority of imperfections successfully; any imperfections that remain are intentionally left to preserve the state of such historical works.

"THE SCHOLAR AS PREACHER"

(THIRD SERIES)

IN THE DAY OF THE ORDEAL

IN THE DAY
OF THE ORDEAL

Sermons

BY

W. P. PATERSON, D.D.

PROFESSOR OF DIVINITY IN THE UNIVERSITY OF EDINBURGH
CHAPLAIN-IN-ORDINARY TO THE KING IN SCOTLAND

SECOND EDITION

EDINBURGH : T. & T. CLARK, 38 George Street

1917

TO

MY WIFE

AND IN MEMORY OF OUR SONS

R. S. PATERSON

SECOND LIEUTENANT, ROYAL FIELD ARTILLERY

NEUVE CHAPELLE

11TH MARCH 1915

W. P. PATERSON

CAPTAIN, KING'S OWN SCOTTISH BORDERERS

DELVILLE WOOD

30TH JULY 1916

PREFACE TO THE SECOND EDITION.

SINCE the last sermon of the present series was preached it has become ever clearer that this is a war, not merely of conflicting interests, but even more of antagonistic principles and types of faith. Moreover, while in the first months the war seemed to be most aptly described as the humiliation of Christ, the period has increasingly taken on the features of "one of the days of the Son of Man." We can now think of Him, not so much or chiefly, as the Man of Sorrows weeping over a maddened and desolated Christendom, interceding that these days should be shortened lest no flesh be saved, but rather as executing offices of government which the Scriptures ascribe to the Son of Man as the instrument of God's transactions with mankind. He has been coming again as the Judge, who is trying each nation's thought and work of what sort they are, and who is either pronouncing upon them His well-done, or exposing them to shame and contempt. He is returning in the character accepted by Him in the Synagogue of Nazareth, when it was declared that He was sent "to proclaim liberty to the captives and the opening of the prison to them that are bound." We have already seen something of the breaking of yokes, and we shall doubtless witness more. Finally, the Son of Man

v

2223184

is returning, if by surprising ways, to do His work of reconciliation by promoting the unity of the nations which God made of one blood.   As an offset to the fierce disruption in the European family, we have seen the hereditary feud with France replaced by a romantic friendship; while the American Commonwealth, girding on its armour in the spirit of a Knight of the Round Table, has clasped hands with us, and is preparing to ratify the new compact by the ancient ritual of the covenant-sacrifice.   For the first time in history there has been an uprising of the human race as such in pursuit and defence of the interests of man as man, and of a programme dictated by the universal conscience; and we may well hope that such a confederation will prove, not a passing incident, but a step towards the practical realisation of the brotherhood of the nations.

The sermons here printed are a selection from those preached in St. George's, Edinburgh, in 1915–16, in the absence, on combatant service, of the minister, Captain the Rev. Gavin Lang Pagan.   Things new and old may be noted in them by other congregations to which I have ministered, and which I affectionately call to remembrance—in my former parish of Crieff, in King's College Chapel, Aberdeen, and in the Scots Church, Melbourne.   I am indebted to Messrs. Hodder & Stoughton for permission to reprint from the *British Weekly* the sermon on the " Consecration of our Goods."

W. P. PATERSON.

EDINBURGH, *June* 1917.

CONTENTS.

———◆———

CHAP.   PAGE

    I. In the Day of the Ordeal . . . 1

   II. The Way of God with the Nation . . 17

  III. The Way of God with the Individual , 32

   IV. Our Maker 47

    V. The Magnetism of the Cross . . . 62

   VI. Free Grace 76

  VII. Repentance 88

 VIII. The Recording Books . . . 101

   IX. The Descent into Hell 116

    X. The Presbyterian Heritage . . . 132

   XI. Reverence 147

  XII. Spots on the Love-Feasts . . . 162

 XIII. The Social Mission of the Church . . 179

 XIV. The Consecration of our Goods . . 197

  XV. The Bible-Picture of Woman . . . 212

 XVI. In Quest of Tranquillity . . . 229

XVII. Retrospect and Prospect . . . 244

IN THE DAY OF THE ORDEAL.

I.

IN THE DAY OF THE ORDEAL.

"And half of the mountain shall remove toward the north, and half of it toward the south."—ZECHARIAH xiv. 4.

A STRIKING feature of the topography of Edinburgh is its two main ridges——one fringed by Princes Street, the other crowned by the Castle Rock and sloping down to Holyrood, and the two separated by a deep valley. Geologists tell us of the processes of nature by which this picturesque site was fashioned ——of the volcanic agency that piled up the ridges and the crags, and of the glaciers that, ploughing their way from the uplands to the Firth, scooped out the hollow in which the waters of the North Loch were one day to lie, and which at a later time was to find room for a railroad and to blossom as a garden.

In our text the prophet describes a landscape closely

resembling the familiar scene which has been pictured. He foretold a convulsion which would alter the configuration of the Holy City. This effect was to be produced, not by the slow operation of the forces of nature, but by an immediate manifestation of the power of the Most High. In his vision he beheld God descend upon the Mount of Olives, and rend the mass in twain. " And his feet shall stand in that day upon the mount of Olives, which is before Jerusalem on the east, and the mount of Olives shall cleave in the midst thereof toward the east and toward the west, and there shall be a very great valley ; and half of the mountain shall remove toward the north, and half of it toward the south."

The prediction of Zechariah cannot be taken literally. The Mount of Olives still stands, solid and unriven—its contour practically the same as in the prophet's day. He would doubtless have said himself that he spake in a figure, and the inner meaning was that a providential visitation was at hand which would have the effect of displacing, sifting, and separating the population of Jerusalem. The picture of the great hill cleft in twain, with a deep gorge cut between the two parts, expressed the truth that a catastrophe in the life of a nation has the character of a process of judgment, which acts as a dividing force, extorts vital decisions, and gathers men into their own distinct and characteristic companies. The same observation has been made as to the results of the earthquake which, in our day, has shaken the frame of things, broken up the fountains of the great deep, and filled the earth with anarchy, destruction and lamentation. It is true that, when we consider the life of our people on the large scale, the cataclysm appears to have produced chiefly a unifying effect: it has consolidated as well as revealed the unity of the congeries of peoples who form our Empire, and it has evoked the unaccustomed spectacle of a practical unanimity of the national intellect and of the national will. But when we reflect on the deeper spiritual and moral results, as they appear among individuals and even groups we become conscious that, to borrow the imagery of Zechariah, part of the mountain has removed toward the north, and part toward the south, with a very great valley between.

I.

THE RELIGIOUS CLEAVAGE.

The war has proved to be a dividing force in the realm of religion. A general effect of the upheaval has been to make us lose interest in things of minor importance—such as games, personal gossip, our bodily ailments, and the narrow issues of party politics, and to concentrate our attention on matters which are of vital moment for time or eternity. In these circumstances it was inevitable that religion should once more emerge into the foreground of consciousness, since in such an ordeal nothing can be more important than to decide whether our Christian gospel is, as it claims, the most valuable of human possessions or the most pathetic of human illusions. The outcome has been that some have told us that they have weighed in the balances the Bible, the Christian revelation, even God Himself, and—God help them !—have found them wanting; while to others their faith, with its gracious aids and its supernatural hopes, has become even more certain and precious than before.

1. There are those who, having now begun to do some thinking on the subject, have discovered that they do not really believe what they formerly assented to in instinctive deference to custom or tradition; and there are others who, having previously made shipwreck of their faith, have felt impelled, by the fresh evidence that ours is a God-forsaken world, to proclaim their unbelief from the housetops. These opinions have found utterance in articles in reviews and magazines and in newspaper correspondence, they have been debated in many a conversation in camp and club, and most ministers have met with echoes and fruits of the controversies during the discharge of the increasingly difficult duties of the pastoral office. When we ask for the reason of the loss of faith, we find that in substance the sceptical contention is the reproduction of a famous old-world argument which is known as the Epicurean dilemma. Applied to the present calamity the argument runs thus : " God was either unable to prevent the occurrence of this terrible war, or He was unwilling; if He was not able to prevent it, He is not omnipotent; if He was able, but would not, He is not

good." Some have chosen one horn of the dilemma, some the other. A very thoughtful and pithy writer who initiated a correspondence on religion and the war gave up the divine omnipotence: he was inclined to believe that there is a God who wishes us well, and who seeks to do us good, but he was of opinion that—possibly because of the cunning and strength of a realm of evil, of which the Devil is the symbol—He is prevented from giving practical effect to His kindly intentions. In an article in the *Nineteenth Century* a well-known public man supported the other alternative, and marshalled a band of witnesses, representative of different classes, who generally agreed that the war proves that there is no God who looks down in compassion on the world, and who cares for the weak and the oppressed, and for little children. What is the reply from the Christian standpoint? Briefly, it is that God, because He is benevolent, conferred upon man the dignity of a free being, with power to choose between good and evil; and that, although He is omnipotent, even the Almighty could not do the two contradictory things of giving man freedom, and also not giving him freedom. One may or may not draw a triangle, but if he does he must accept the consequences that the angles will be equal to two right angles; and similarly it was possible for God either to create or not to create such a being as man, but if He did, He had to accept him with all that was involved in his being man, including the possibility that he would misconceive his own true end, and break the moral laws of the universe. We should probably all agree that it is better to be a man than a sheep, though a sheep has no vices and commits no crimes. That it is possible for a benevolent being to think a perilous freedom a greater good than a fettered safety appears from the fact that a father may love a son as his own soul, and yet allow him to choose a career which has the possibility of issuing, not merely in success and happiness, but also in failure and tragedy. There is, further, a fairly close analogy between the providential arrangement of permitting evil for the sake of a greater good and the principles which govern the action of the earthly power which we call the State. We find that under the rule of the State there prevails a great deal of deplorable vice—drunkenness, gambling, impurity in its many debasing and destructive forms, and also a great deal of suffering due to unjust and inhumane dealing between man and man; and so long as the evil actions fall short of crime the State does not greatly interfere. But we do not therefore argue that the State is either indifferent to the well-being of the community, or that (should it wish to do so) it is powerless to stamp out vice and inhumanity. We give it credit for desiring to promote the general moral well-being, and we recognise that, if it cared to exercise its power, it could prohibit and punish almost every form of wickedness. But it generally proceeds, and with general approval, on the view that it is better to leave to individuals a very large measure of personal freedom—even if many abuse it to their destruction—rather than to get rid of the evils by guiding society by force into the ways of respectability and the paths of virtue. It is not apparent why men should think that it is the sensible and practical course for an earthly government to pay as much respect as possible to individual liberty, and that, in so far as the divine government acts on similar principles, it should be declared to be either impotent, or indifferent to human well-being.

There is, however, it is to be noted, another side to the providential government of the world. Just as the State, while generally respecting individual liberty, has its measures of coercion and restraint, so God reserves to Himself a degree of control over the evil forces which pollute, distract, and ravage the world. He at least sets bounds to the range and destructiveness of wickedness—even as in the natural sphere there is a limit to the possibilities of the tempest and the earthquake; and, above all, He takes measures to ensure that the calamities which He permits will on the whole and in the end be overruled for good. An earthly government experiments and hopes; God sees past the scandals and the failures to the end, and permits and tolerates the evils because of His knowledge that the drama of human affairs will eventually have an issue that will be the more splendidly worthy both of man and of God.

2. While the faith of some has been shaken, the faith of more has been deepened and confirmed by the experiences through which we have recently passed.

The portion of the mountain on the south side is by far the more densely populated. There are some who, in spite of the present appearances of a chaotic universe, have taken long views of history, and acquired a stronger conviction than before that the Lord, while paying respect to human freedom, overrules all for His own ends in the long-run. Europe was the better in the long-run, and not the worse, for the French Revolution. England is what it is to-day because of events which once seemed sheer calamities—an Anglo-Saxon invasion, a Norman conquest, the civil war of the seventeenth century. Many even think that they can trace the hand of a wise and considerate Providence in the chequered experiences of their individual lot. Still more is there a widespread and deep-seated conviction that the grace of God is sufficient for the worst of the distresses and the fears which afflict the souls of men and women in this evil time. These are not, so much as might have been expected, identical with those who have wholly escaped the calamities of the war: many of them have entered into the fellowship of Christ's sufferings, and have acquired a fresh understanding of the meaning of Gethsemane and Calvary. But they have also become more assured than before of the truth of the promise, "Lo, I am with you alway, even unto the end of the world"; they have proved that there is a strength which is made perfect in weakness and a grace which makes even the evil things to work together for their good; and they know that it is not an empty phrase that speaks of a peace of God, passing understanding, which the world can neither give nor take away.

II.

THE MORAL CLEAVAGE.

While the ordeal of the war has been trying religious faith, it has been even more of a sifting and dividing force in the moral sphere. There is a conviction, and on the whole it is well founded, that the war has separated the European nations into two groups—of which one has been animated by a spirit of ambitious and calculated aggression, and has accepted the immoral principle that might determines right, while the other group has been challenged to fight in self-defence, and retains the traditional civilised prejudice in favour of a code of international morality. When we consider the behaviour of our own people as a whole, we find that it has been on a satisfactorily, and even a surprisingly, high level. Those who believed that, in spite of many enervating and corrupting influences, the heart of the people was sound, and its strength unsapped, have found much to justify their faith—in the decisiveness with which the nation acted from the day when the threat to its interests was reinforced by the appeal to its chivalry, in its prompt resolution to throw the whole of its manhood and of its wealth into the scales, in its calling of a truce to the conflicts and the intrigues of

party spirit, in its splendid response to the calls
for service in the care of the stricken, and in the
replenishment of the manifold streams of human
kindness and of Christian charity.   But, after all, the
nation is made up of individuals, and the war has
had the effect, not only of revealing, but also of
exaggerating, the amazing moral differences which
exist within the compass of our common human nature,
and which represent every shade of moral quality
from the loftiest heights of sacrifice to the lowest
depths of selfishness and depravity.   The parable of
Zechariah is re-enacted, and we seem to see " one half
of the mountain remove toward the north, and half of
it toward the south."   Let us note three of the more
striking contrasts.

1. There is, first, the contrast between the cult of
patriotism and the service of Mammon.   It might
have been expected that, with so great a multitude of
our men making willing sacrifice of business and
career, of health and life, and our womanhood
heroically sharing in the sacrifice, the worship of
Mammon would have fallen altogether into disrepute,
and that at least for the time being money would
have been counted as dross.   But the force of habit
has proved too strong.   There are those in whose
breasts the passion of avarice seems even to have been
inflamed rather than suppressed by the new conditions, and who have shown themselves even less
scrupulous than before in their haste to be rich.   As
if it were not sufficient to make profit out of the

extraordinary demands of a time of war, it has been revealed in official papers that there was a somewhat widespread desire to overreach and even to swindle the Government in Army contracts; and when we inquire as to the alarming increase in the price of bread, we are informed in passionless financial papers that a contributory cause was that there were large operators who forestalled supplies of wheat, and held them back in the expectation of selling them at famine prices. Nor is it only one class that has incurred the reproach of serving Mammon rather than country. In the earlier stages of the war there were strikes in mine and factory which were no doubt partly due to the fact that the workers believed the capitalists to be claiming an inequitable share of the wealth which was being wrung out of the needs of our people, but which were also due to the feeling that the opportunity was too good to be lost of furthering the material interests of a section at the expense of the community. To the credit of the labouring classes it has to be added that with the progress of the war the appeal to their sense of patriotic duty has prevailed more and more over the selfish instinct, and that they have made surrenders of hard-won privileges which claim the outsider's hearty admiration.

2. A second contrast is that between self-sacrifice and self-indulgence. Side by side with the self-forgetting offerings of men and women, of which we have spoken, there has persisted the old conception of

life as being ours that we may seek our own comfort, ease, and pleasure. The impression got by those who are interested in the War Savings movement is that there are many who think that, being better off than they ever were before, they are entitled for once in a way to take their share of the good things of this life. This view is of course largely accounted for by ignorance of the temporary and illusory character of the present prosperity, but it is also a consequence and fruit of the low theory of life, which in time past has been fostered and encouraged by all classes, according to which the last word is that a man may do what he will with his own, and that the best use is to try to procure with it what will pass for happiness. The deliberate pursuit of pleasure still fills far too large a space in the general life of the nation. It is true that the class, or rather the section of a class, which formerly made a business of pleasure, has been very radically reformed, and has largely rediscovered the superior blessedness of engaging in work which is of acknowledged benefit to society ; but it appears from recent sumptuary regulations that there are some rich people who have not yet realised that there is a limit beyond which luxury becomes scandalous. The spurious and deceptive prosperity of the times has led to a great increase of spending power in wide circles of the community, and the ampler means are very generally made use of for entertainment and enjoyment. One need not be of a morose or fanatical temper to feel that it is unbecoming, and worse, that in the most critical and perhaps tragical year of our nation's history there should still be so much frivolity, and the land should resound with the noise of merry-making and even of revelry. The other day I heard an outburst of cheering which would have worthily celebrated the relief of Bukharest or the fall of Trieste, and it turned out that the occasion only was that a popular football club had secured a goal in a keenly contested match. Recreation does something for efficiency ; but it does not strike an observer as a symptom of the will to victory that—to take an item from the news of the day—music halls are paying unexampled dividends, and that "the salaries of the artistes are soaring by leaps and bounds, and there seems to be no finality in sight." It is a curious paradox that, while the extremes of self-sacrifice cast a spell upon mind and will, the ingrained selfishness asserts itself when the call to self-denial concerns itself merely with the far less important questions as to what we shall eat, and what we shall drink, and wherewithal we shall be clothed. As regards eating, there are many who have failed to grasp the element-ary moral principle that the question is, not what kind of dinner they can afford to pay for, but whether they are entitled to eat so much when there is barely enough to go round, and when their extra demand helps to force up prices and make it difficult for others to get a meal at all. As regards drinking, it will seem to future ages a curious psychological problem that the same people which meekly accepted compulsion when its men were called upon to face the worst risks of the most destructive war in history should be considered by the Scottish Secretary to be so wedded to alcoholic liquor that there would be danger of the gravest labour troubles if its patriotism were put to the crucial test of imposing total abstinence during the period of the war. It is to be hoped that the number and the influence of those making this threat has been exaggerated; but there is at least reason to think that prohibition, even if declared to be an economic necessity, would provoke more violent opposition than anything else which has been done in the restriction of our liberty, or even in claiming our money for public uses.

3. A third and darker contrast to the moral nobility of the time is furnished by the persistence, and even the development, of flagrant vices. Respectable society cultivates the habit of ignoring as far as possible the extent and range of the vices, especially of the worst sins of the flesh, which even in ordinary times poison the life of our people, sap its strength, and every year slay their thousands and their tens of thousands; it contents itself with a vague general belief that there has been steady if slow improvement in all respects; and it has a feeling that, if we think of moral evils at all in these days, it should only be to consider the splendid atonement which has been made for past misdeeds by many of the sinners, and to throw over the national vices the cloak of Christian charity. But we do not get rid of the facts and

their consequences by shutting our eyes to them, nor
does the ministry of charity sufficiently dispose of
them. It is certain that the war has supplied fuel,
not only to the enthusiasms and the heroisms of the
soul, but also to the destroying lusts of the flesh;
and if its most characteristic products are the man
who found his soul in renouncing self and the world,
and the woman who has been tried as gold in the
furnace, it has also by-products in many a new-
found victim of the old-established vices that prey
upon the life of our cities, and most pathetically in the
instance of the wife who will welcome back a husband
—should he return to his own—to a home of misery
and shame.

No doubt there are many who would say that they
are not conscious that the war has made much
difference in themselves, either spiritually or morally.
But as a fact they are not where they were before.
They may be half-way between the part of the
mountain which removed to the north, and the
part of it which removed to the south, but, as in
Zechariah's vision, the intermediate space in which
they stand has sunk to a lower level. Not to have
changed is to be relatively worse than before. It is
impossible to live through a great time without acting
either greatly or meanly, even if to act greatly it is not
necessary that we should do or attempt great things,
but only that we should be filled and guided by the
right spirit. A time like this, the prophets taught, is

a day of the Lord which has the function of a day of
Judgment, and it has placed each of us on our trial.
The fundamental religious test is : Do we hold fast
our faith in God, and believe that, though clouds and
thick darkness are round about Him, He has shined
upon us in Jesus Christ, and given us to trust His
wisdom and His love?   The fundamental moral
test is whether the centre of gravity has shifted in
our lives, and we have learned to ask, not where we
can find profit or pleasure, but how we can be of
some use.   Let us ask our conscience to apply these
tests and deliver a verdict.   Self-knowledge is difficult, but the conscience has moments of insight in
which it wonderfully justifies its title of the Vice-
gerent of God.   Amen.

THE WAY OF GOD WITH THE NATION.

"The Lord God hath spoken, who can but prophesy?"—AMOS
iii. 8.

THE General Assembly of the Church of Scotland
recently appointed a Commission on the spiritual
and moral issues of the war. The instructions given
to the Commission were wide and far-reaching, and
its labours will doubtless issue in a national mission
with a comprehensive religious and ethical programme. Among other directions the Assembly
advised that steps be taken to forward the understanding of the things which God has been speaking
from heaven through the visitation of the war, and
it suggested that the Presbyteries of the Church
should meet in conference and seek for more light
upon this deep and solemn subject. It was my
privilege to be present at one of the first of these
conferences, and this sermon is the outcome of
reflection on what was then said, and of the inter-
change of thought with my brethren on the great
providential theme.

The scene of conference was well suited to a

2

meditation on war and peace. The place of meeting
was a sequestered village, which nestles at the foot
of a range of hills bordering the upper valley of
the Forth, and which looks across a broad plain to
the towering masses of the Grampians. The panorama
that spread out before us reminded us how much
of the story of Scotland has been the chronicle of
wars. The distant Bens that guard the region of
the Trossachs, and Stirling with its river that " bridled
the wild Highlanders," recalled the ancient feud and
the bloody reprisals of the Gael and the Sassenach.
There were the landmarks also, in the Wallace
Monument and the castled crag of Stirling, of the
more famous conflict in which Lowlander and
Highlander were comrades in arms, and threw off
the yoke of the English kingdom. A mansion in
the neighbourhood, in which Prince Charlie once
dined and slept, brought back the year in which
Scotland last knew " the shock and furious close of
civil butchery." Of the present struggle there was a
reminder in the aircraft which hovered like giant
birds over the Carse, and, exulting in their wings (as
Homer says), rose and dipped in the air, and headed
for their nests. But there, too, were evidences that
war is an episode in the history of nations, and that
their settled habit is peace. The broad strath which
lay at our feet, once a waste of swamp and bog, had
long since been reclaimed by human industry and
skill, and with its teeming cornfields and its tinted
orchards it seemed beautiful, in the sunny glimpses

of the summer morning, as a garden of the Lord. The atmosphere was like that of a Sabbath, falling in the midst of the reign of the Prince of Peace, as we wended our way, a goodly company of ministers, to the village church on the tree-clad slope, and after a lesson from a prophet and a prayer in the name and the spirit of Christ, we took up the first part of our duty, and essayed to trace the hand of the Almighty in the dark dispensation of the world-war.

I.

THE SECULAR VOICE.

We may first consider the purely secular explanation. Many are satisfied with finding second causes, and disclaim the assumption of a higher purpose. The only explanation which need be looked for, they say, is that a great nation felt the need of more breathing-space and elbow-room, and that the impulse arising from its wants was intensified by its ambition. Germany has a population of 70,000,000, which has been increasing at the rate of 1,000,000 a year; it was driven by a natural necessity to seek new outlets and additional means of subsistence; a very intelligible sentiment made it wish to have colonies in which its sons would remain German in blood and speech; its exaggerated sense of its greatness led it to form extravagant dreams of dominating Europe, and building up a new world-Empire; its unparalleled military strength gave it confidence to embark on a career of conquest; and the present European chaos is the result of its collision with other nations which were no less vitally interested in opposing and frustrating its designs. The war, in short, was what was to be expected of human nature under the afore-mentioned conditions, at least if to need, cupidity, and opportunity we add the dangerous ingredients of national vanity and a morbid suspiciousness and anxiety for the future; and to go in quest of a higher purpose, which even from the religious point of view has often been thought to be presumptuous, may well appear to the ordinary man to be foolish and fruitless.

The kind of explanation which is offered by the secular voice is, of course, essential to the understanding of historical events, but it is not exclusive of the supplementary explanation of a higher providential purpose. In the ordinary affairs of life men perform many actions which are dictated by private motives, and directed to narrow personal advantages; and their doings are nevertheless embraced in, and are made contributory to, larger schemes, which may lie outside of their intentions and even of their knowledge. In a great city, for example, we see multitudes of persons going about their daily business, and scarcely conscious of working for anything save their own interests, or those of their dependents; while yet the outcome of the haphazard self-seeking is that they are fitted fairly well into the social mechanism, and that they help to make, not indeed an ideal, but at least a surprisingly effective, provision for meeting the numerous and complex wants of the community. Perhaps an even more impressive illustration is the way in which a presiding Providence, working through passions and instincts which are themselves blind, takes order for the perpetuation of the human race, and for the suitable education of the units of the successive generations. When a building is erected we do not suppose that the whole process is explained by giving a list of the workmen who have had a hand in the labour, and showing what reward each expected for his work. The still more important agents are the person or persons who desired that a building of a particular kind should be erected, and the architect who was entrusted with the design. And similarly it is very conceivable, and indeed most credible, that the temple of humanity, though reared by human hands, originated in the mind of a master-builder, has progressed under His direction, and will one day be finished in accordance with His plan.

But here the secular voice protests: "The analogy of the building is more damaging than helpful. There may be some evidence of a mind at work on a large scale, but those who erect houses do not arrange to have the work interrupted. It does not enter into their designs to contrive that dissension will break out among the workmen, or that these will deface and even destroy the edifice which they are employed to erect." This is obviously true; but the analogy helps us to understand how God might at least foresee and permit the evil without thereby ceasing to be the master-mind of history. The human builder may foresee that there will be trouble among the workmen, and may nevertheless resolve to proceed with the work in the expectation that the difficulties will be overcome, and that the plans will in the long-run be executed to his satisfaction; and similarly it is entirely credible that God should have begun and should carry on His work notwithstanding His knowledge that there would be occasional episodes of rebellion and outrage. Furthermore, it is now generally agreed that an employer is better served by a body of free workmen, even if their liberty may assert itself disastrously, than by a gang of slaves; and it is similarly believable that God will eventually win a nobler result from a world of free human beings, even if they occasionally perpetrate the most insensate acts, than He would have secured from a world of beings who rendered Him mechanical obedience and service. In the light of the analogy of the builder we can therefore see reasons why God should have permitted and accepted the conditions of human life from which the present catastrophe has sprung; and further, since God's interest in mankind is much more intimate and many-sided than that of an employer of labour, we may reasonably suppose that He has some other purpose which is served in His permission of such a visitation. What are we to say of this further purpose?

II.

THE RETRIBUTIVE THEORY.

At this point a second voice strikes into the debate. It is the voice of Amos of Tekoah, of John the Baptist, of the Scottish Covenanter. Its fundamental certainty is that the tragedy of the war, while rooted on the earthly side in human wickedness, is in a real sense the act of God; and it feels no greater dubiety as to the meaning and purpose of the appalling visitation. The war, with the sufferings which it involves, is the judgment of God upon the sins of the nations of Europe: by reason of their love of the world, their carnal excesses, their covetousness, their pride, and their ungodliness, they have provoked the wrath of the Almighty, so that He has returned to trample them in His fury, to drench the earth with their blood, and to fill their homes with woe and lamentation. For our own country, the accuser proceeds, the providential dispensation has the same intention. We have provoked God by our heinous national sins, the guilt of which is aggravated by the unique favours and privileges enjoyed by our people; and out of the darkness and the whirlwind there comes to us the call to repent of our sins, if haply it be not too late, and to implore of the avenging

Judge that in the midst of wrath He would remember mercy.

This voice is entitled to a most respectful hearing—and not merely because it is in this way that our spiritual ancestors might have construed the situation, and appealed for support to the Old Testament. Such an explanation at least founds upon a fact which is not open to question—namely, that the war, regarded in its broadest aspect, is the consequence and the penalty of human wickedness and folly. It is because Europe, while Christian in name, has remained essentially pagan in its public policy—its nations on the whole following the natural lusts, and only playing with the principle of human brotherhood, that the Continent which was the chosen home of civilisation has been transformed into a chaos and an Inferno. We are also manifestly being punished for the failings of the rulers of the earth. It will seem incredible to a later age that there was not enough wisdom in the diplomacy of Europe to come to some arrangement which would have averted the catastrophe. It does not appear that the general situation was ever thoroughly discussed by those who were responsible for controlling it. Our own leaders have their full share of responsibility. If they had told our people to prepare, or rather compelled them to prepare, to use the full might of Britain in self-defence and on the side of righteousness in the event of aggression, there would probably have been no war ; and their only plea is—and this can be said of both political parties—that they were either too ignorant and blind to see what was coming, or that they had not the courage to propound a policy of national armament which would be likely to prove unpopular at a General Election. But can we take the further step, as the prophetic voice urges, of declaring the war to be the punishment of our national sins—as drunkenness, impurity, profanity, religious indifference, and such-like? What is true is that sins are always being punished, and that because of our many and flagrant national sins, the life of our people has been considerably weakened and tainted, and its hands have been less strong than they otherwise would have been for grappling with the heavy business of war. But there was as good reason for saying that God was afflicting us for our sins in 1913, as there is for saying that He is punishing us in 1916, and there is no reason for regarding the calamities of the war as a more direct and special measure of retribution. We are being punished for our sins, inasmuch as we are always being punished for them, but we are not to think of ourselves as the victims of a heaped-up and retarded vengeance. The general mind refuses to accept the theory of a special penal judgment, and it has a justification. When our nation entered the war, we hold with a good conscience, it followed a call of duty, and put aside a temptation to which it would have been easy to yield—the temptation to avoid the appalling risks, spare the lives of our fellow-countrymen, and gather riches out of the agony of the Continent. It therefore seems more just, as well as more charitable, to say that our calamities are on the whole sufferings which have overtaken us because we were found in the way of righteousness, rather than that they come from the vials of wrath which God has poured out upon the heads of our people because of their multiplied and impenitent wickedness.

III.

THE REMEDIAL THEORY.

Here, accordingly, the third voice takes up the argument. It is the same voice which, by the mouth of Elihu, declared to the patriarch Job that the purpose of his sufferings was, not to expose and punish a wicked man, but to make a good man a better man. It also has support in the teaching of those Old Testament prophets who declared that while God in His anger chastised the nation for its sins, He selected those forms of chastisement which were likely to make of Israel a holy and righteous nation. The distinctive feature of its message is that the essential providential purpose of the war is that it may be a means of blessing to our people, by the purification and ennoblement of its character and life.

"Who does not feel to-day," it proceeds, " that our people as a whole has risen in the scale of moral dignity? In our national history there has been much that seems merely calculating if not sordid: to the end of time this chapter of our history will shine with the lustre of an heroic age which shrank from no sacrifice, and which thought less of self-interest than of duty and chivalry. A moral regeneration is traceable among all classes : it has been realised, as never before, that the self-centred life is as unworthy as it is unproductive of happiness. Commonplace souls have risen to heights of grandeur in action and suffering. Sympathy has been born or reborn in many a callous or hardened heart. Many who had been living without God, and without any vision of the things that lie beyond the senses, have awakened to the reality of the unseen and eternal world, and have groped their way back from the far country to the eternal home of the soul."

To many the message of this comforter may not seem wholly convincing. He has shut his eyes, they say, to one-half of the facts. "Was it a blessing that millions of men were torn from their peaceful and beneficent occupations, and hurled back into the conditions of savagery—with anger, suspicion, and hatred as governing impulses, and the maiming and slaying of men as their trade ? Is it common sense to say that the nation is substantially improved by an event which is sweeping away tens if not hundreds of thousands of men who were the flower of their generation and the hope of the future ? And is there not an incalculable moral loss ? In a world in which everything has been turned upside down, how easy must it seem to many to dispense with the guiding principles even of elementary morality. How many

souls have been blasted and destroyed by despair!
How many have sought forgetfulness or relief in the
consolations of the flesh! How many have been
tempted to curse God and die!" The rejoinder is
weighty, and it is a seasonable corrective of the
optimistic sentimentalism which asks to have all for the
very best. Though the third voice is right in affirming that our people as a whole has been lifted by the
war to a higher plane, the tale of loss is so heavy that
we feel something more to be wanting by way of
compensation for the tremendous sacrifices, moral as
well as material, which have accompanied the partial
regeneration. And this brings us to the cognate, but
really supplementary, message of the last interpreter.

IV.

THE CALL TO NEW TASKS.

The meaning of the visitation, says the fourth voice,
is that it comes as the dawning day of new opportunities. The purpose is, not merely that we may
become better, but that better things may be done.
It may even be that many are sacrificed in soul as
well as in body, to the end that a brighter day may
be ushered in. Future historians will probably date a
new epoch from the world-war of the twentieth century.
It doubtless marks the beginning of the end of the
chronic curse of war; for it has been demonstrated
that war has become not merely too horrible, but also

too expensive, to be a permanent institution of our earth. If the present struggle is to be the operation that is to remove the deadly disease which has afflicted the race from its infancy, it does not seem, from the point of view of general history, that the fee was too heavy for the cure. It is also to be expected that after the war a stronger faith will be cherished in the possibility of coping with other malignant evils. We have learned what a great people can do when it devotes itself with one heart and mind to the organisation of victory; and it will seem a matter of course that the same energy, earnestness, and method should be applied to the perennial warfare with ignorance and destitution, vice and crime, and that the spirit of brotherhood, so signally exemplified in arms, should be equally realised in the arts and the avocations of peace. The Church for its part, we hope, will see things in new proportion and perspective, and will forget many ancient controversies in the light of the tasks of the present and the future. To many an individual it has come and will come with the haunting message of Robertson of Brighton: "There is a past that is beyond recall, but there is a future that is still our own."

The conclusion of the matter may be taken to be that God, while not directly the author of the visitation which has come upon the earth—else were His Kingdom divided against itself—yet has it sufficiently under the direction of His permitting and controlling

will to entitle us to speak of it as coming within the
scope of His effective government; and further, that
the wisdom of the Infinite Being is so great that He
is able to make use of one and the same means to
accomplish several and diverse ends.   In and through
the one visitation He is punishing, regenerating, and
issuing a summons to fresh and higher tasks, and the
only question open to discussion is as to the chief end
which He has in view in permitting these troubles.
There is an analogous problem in the human sphere
in regard to the meaning of the action of society in
its treatment of criminals.   It imposes upon those
who break its laws a painful discipline of restraints
and penalties, while yet it is able so to contrive this
discipline that to a real extent it fulfils the three
purposes of protecting society, exacting a satisfaction
to justice, and effecting some improvement in the
wrong-doer.   It remains, however, matter of debate—
and has, as a fact, been much debated—which of the
three ends is that which it has primarily in view.
The human and the divine government thus agree in
pursuing several ends in dealing with wrong-doers, but
in my judgment their chief end is different.   With an
earthly government the protection of society is the chief
concern, while under the government of God we seem
justified in holding that the dominant and persistent
purpose, even in most of the judgments which have
an apparent character of final retribution, is to compass
the amendment of the offender and increase his powers
and opportunities of serving God and advancing His

Kingdom. We cannot doubt of His retributive justice, but we can also believe that retribution is merely the form which divine love is compelled to assume when it takes counsel with divine wisdom as to the proper response to the challenge of human wickedness.

It is by a combination of gifts of grace with penal judgments that the Ruler of History has normally guided and seconded human progress, and the common root of both has been the wise love of the Eternal. This has been amply illustrated in former centuries in the history of our own people, which has not only been highly favoured by unmerited Providential gifts, but has had striking experience of the alchemy of Providence that can change even the merited curse into a blessing. And though doubtless the mind of Providence takes far wider and longer views than open up to our most broad-minded patriotism, in the light of the past we may well take courage to hold that God sets considerable value on our British stock as one of His earthly instruments, and that the wisdom of His love is the key to the understanding, even in the present grievous dispensation, of the way of God with our nation.

Amen.

III.

THE WAY OF GOD WITH THE INDIVIDUAL.

"The very hairs of your head are all numbered."—MATTHEW x. 30.

THE name of Providence does not accurately or at least fully describe what theology understands by God's works of Providence. The word does not of itself carry us further than the truth, important as it is, that God has knowledge and foresight of the wants of His creatures, and makes provision for the supply of their needs. The doctrine of Providence, as commonly expounded by theologians, includes three assertions as to the activity of God in relation to His creatures. It is affirmed that He is their preserver, to whom they owe day by day, directly as well as indirectly, their continued existence. It is also usually affirmed that as the God of Providence He co-operates so closely and constantly with all inanimate forces and with all living creatures as to supply the driving power of all which happens in the Universe—except in so far as events are traceable to the initiative of sinful wills. The third part of the doctrine is that God effectively governs all His creatures and all their actions by the exercise of His almighty power, and in accordance with His wisdom and holiness. The objects of this powerful, wise, and holy administration, it is taught, are co-extensive with the created universe, and when we fasten our attention upon the earth His government is held to embrace the human race as a whole, the nations, the Church, and, lastly, the individual human being.

That there is a divine power which upholds us in being, and which is the light of our seeing, and the strength of our labours, has not been questioned by any considerable body of thinking men. We believe thus much if we believe in God at all. Misgivings begin when it is further asserted that God exercises an effective government over the nations of the earth. The misfortunes of kingdoms and empires have always provoked doubts as to the rule of God in history. Even in the Old Testament we read of scoffers who, when the storm burst upon Israel or Judah, complained that God was invisible and that He did nothing. When the Roman Empire was broken in pieces by the northern barbarians, a great apostasy from the Christian faith was threatened on the ground that the Christian God seemed to have been unable to protect the interests of His wor-shippers. The Scotland of the seventeenth century produced, not only martyrs, but sceptics who were restrained by Parliament from " reasoning against the Providence of God in the government of the world."

Still more widespread have been the doubts as to whether the individual life is embraced in a wise and benevolent scheme of divine rule. In ordinary times it is usually possible to feel that a nation as such lives in the enjoyment of the bounty and the protection of Heaven; but even under normal conditions it is harassed by the arrows that fly by day, and by the pestilence that walketh in darkness, and there are tragedies enough in families and in individual lives which are not easily fitted into the view that God cares for the people one by one. Especially in a time like the present, when the cosmos of the civilised world has been changed into a chaos, and dreams of human progress have been rudely disturbed; when, moreover, the customary damage wrought on earth by the natural forces of destruction has been enormously aggravated and accelerated by the far-reaching ravages of an unparalleled war; it is not surprising that many should be asking if there is really a divine government which, in any rational and intelligent fashion, takes to do with the affairs of mankind.

In this sermon we shall confine our attention to a single branch of the doctrine—the idea of Providence as embracing the individual man, woman, and child. Our subject will be ourselves and our lives, considered as objects of the knowledge, the protection, and the ministrations of an almighty, an all-wise, and a benevolent Deity. We shall first give reasons for believing it to be a fact that we are comprehended in a scheme of divine government which takes particular account of us as individuals, and thereafter we shall raise the more difficult question as to the purpose pursued by God in His providential dealings with us.

I.

THE FACT OF PROVIDENCE.

That Providence deals particularly with individual lives is one of the most distinctive elements of our Lord's teaching. The religious thinkers of the Greek and Roman world could write eloquently about Providence, but they supposed that it had done its work in making a wise and bountiful provision for the welfare of the human race as such, and they conceived it to be beneath the dignity of the Supreme Being to concern Himself about inconsiderable persons and trivial affairs. Jesus taught that God draws no such distinctions, and that He watches over one individual soul with as much solicitude as if He were dealing with a chosen people, or with a line of kings. He encouraged us to think of God as able and willing to do for each of us everything that is prompted by the instincts of a perfect parental love. Like a Father, He said, He knows each of us, loves us, forgives us being penitent; and He also provides for us, protects us, educates us, disciplines us, and destines us to a son's final inheritance. From the one detail of our text we see how particular was His conception of the operations of the Providence of the Heavenly Father—"The hairs of your head are all numbered."

For a Christian the authority of Jesus settles the fact that our lives are embraced in a scheme of particular providences. As Son of God, He came to reveal God; and as the doctrine of God's providential care for us lies at the very core of our Lord's message, we may well regard the announcement as one of the great discovered secrets of the universe. Two additional considerations may be adduced as fitted to confirm our faith that the individual is the object of the special knowledge and the peculiar care of the Almighty. The first is that such a concentration of effort is certainly possible for the Being whose power and wisdom are infinite. God is not too great to trouble Himself with anything so small as our little life: rather is He too great not to do it. The God of infinite power and wisdom is certainly not so preoccupied and burdened with the government of His vast dominions, and with His scheme of universal history, as to be unable to give time and thought to the details of His administration. He is not like an earthly king or prime minister who must devolve on subordinates a great part of his work and responsibility. A second reason for believing in a particular Providence is that man is a being of sufficient value to bespeak the special care of the Supreme Being. From God man derives his existence, in God's image He is made; and God cannot but regard as a thing of priceless worth the human soul on which He stamped the lineaments of His own perfections. Still more deeply may we be impressed with the importance of every individual human being if we take seriously the doctrine that man is the heir of immortality. When we reflect that one human being, if he lives for ever, will traverse during that unending existence a period exceeding in duration the sum of the years that all men now alive will spend upon this planet, and also that his experiences in eternity will exceed in volume and in variety the collective earthly experiences of all who now inhabit the earth, it is not difficult to believe that God puts upon each of us the value which Christ assigned to us when He declared that "the very hairs of your head are all numbered."

II.

THE DESIGNS OF PROVIDENCE.

If now it be a fact that our individual lives are embraced and in some measure controlled by a providential government, the divine rule must work with a programme and towards some definite result. Every form of government implies an end which it pursues. There is a government of the nation, of the family, of the school; and in each of these spheres the ruling power is prepared to give an account of what it aims at doing for those who are subject to its authority. And so the second question arises, Can we trace a leading idea, can we show a fairly consistent purpose, in the way in which the lot of individual men and women is influenced by the system of providential government? Or must we confess that, even though we have faith to believe the fact, the meaning and the purpose of the dealings of Providence with us are shrouded in impenetrable mystery?

There are three interpretations of the plan of Providence in its contact with individual lives which in different periods have entered deeply into religious thinking. Two of these explanations contain elements of truth, but cannot be accepted as complete statements of the design of the providential discipline by which we are beset behind and before. The third I partly believe on evidence, and wholly accept as matter of faith.

1. It is a very ancient and widespread idea that the purpose of Providence—the end which it pursues if there be a Providence at all—is to look after our happiness. Happiness, as commonly understood, rests upon our possession of health and wealth, of home and kin and friends; and it is commonly supposed to be the proper business of Providence to preserve these goods to us amid the perils and changes of this mortal life, and also so to bless our labours that our happiness shall continue to increase. There is reason to think that a very large portion of the human race has valued religion chiefly because it was believed that through the friendship of God we have a guarantee of protection in a world that is ever menacing us with hurt and destruction. And it is undoubtedly true

that God has some interest in our happiness, and in the things which make for happiness. It is the fault, not of Providence, but of ourselves, that most of us are not much happier than we actually are. Moreover, we are taught to pray for protection and for such outward blessings as our daily bread, and there is much evidence that God can, and often does, answer such petitions. At the same time, it is impossible to say that the promotion of happiness is the governing purpose of God in the providential events of the average individual life. When we consider the dark side of human existence—the physical weakness and torment to which the flesh is heir, the failures and the losses which harrow the spirit, the human wreckage with which the world is strewn—we may feel that it is less true that man was made to rejoice than that he was made to mourn, and that while Providence has some care for our temporal well-being, there must be something else for which it cares very much more.

2. A second view, which has played a great part in earnest religious thought, is that the dealings of Providence with the individual are fully accounted for by the principle of retribution. Every event which befalls a man has been supposed to be an act of judgment—the calamities being penalties inflicted for wrong-doing, while success and well-being are interpreted as tokens of the divine approval of piety and virtue. Among the Jews this was the popular belief down to the time of our Lord. The explanation given

in the great religions of India of the staggering inequalities of the individual lot is that they are the
due reward of individual merit or demerit which was
acquired, if not in the present life, at least in a previous state of existence.   The mind of the Scottish
people was formerly possessed by a strong belief in
special judgments, and persons were to be met with in
older generations who were prepared to see a judgment
on a neighbour in a signal reverse of fortune, a stroke
of paralysis, or a premature death in the family.
What makes this view respectable is that those who
hold it have a glimpse of one of the most solemn and
certain of truths—namely, that every sin entails
punishment, that even if it be not found out it finds
out the sinner, and is at least followed by inward and
invisible penalties; and that as a fact the ineffective-
ness, the gloom, and the misery of countless lives are
the direct consequence and punishment of open or
secret sins both of the flesh and of the spirit.   But it
is equally certain that rewards and punishments of the
external and visible kind are not meted out with judicial
exactness in view of worthiness and unworthiness.   The
Book of Job shows that on this point the most believing minds of the Old Testament had become sceptical.
Our Lord expressly repudiated it when He was asked
for the providential explanation of the case of the man
born blind.   In this life there is enough of retribution
to convince us that we live under an order of things
which pays its tribute to the moral laws, but assuredly
the providential dispensation is at most an instalment

and a prediction of the reckoning that we look for at the Last Judgment.

3. The interpretation of the purpose of Providence which agrees with the doctrine of the Fatherhood of God, and which most closely fits the varied facts of ordinary experience, is that our earthly life has the character of a divine education. There is a kind of earthly providence, as has been said, which presides over the life of the school and of the family, and its operations throw light upon the aims and methods of divine Providence. The aim of the training in the family and in the school is educative, and in education two things are attempted. On the one hand it is sought to form the mind and the character of the child according to a good model, and on the other it is sought to give a training which will make him into a useful member of society. And if we conceive that the providential ordering of our lives is directed to one or other or both of these ends—either to make us better or to use us for the good of others, or to do both things, we shall find a clue that enables us, if not to solve all enigmas, at least to smooth away many of the difficulties which beset the doctrine of a particular Providence.

The main purpose of the providential discipline of our lives is, as it has been expressed, to contribute to the making of a soul. The chief end of man is to glorify God by the acquisition of a character made up of the virtues and the graces; the seeds of those qualities are implanted in our souls by the ministries of nature and grace; and the providential events of our lives form a discipline which is designed to carry us onwards towards perfection. From the point of view that our life has an educative purpose, it may become intelligible why we should have meted out to us so diverse experiences of prosperity and adversity, of joy and sorrow. Those who have to do with the training of children know that some can be educated only by being made to endure hardness and severity, while others are influenced only by sympathetic and magnanimous treatment; and similarly it may well be that the Heavenly Father, in seeking to draw out what is best in us, or drive out what is worst, may assign to one class an experience in which they have the feeling of habitually struggling with an unkind destiny, and to another an experience in which they have a sense of being treated as special favourites of the scheme of things. On the other hand there are many persons, probably the majority, who have known both experiences, and whose lives have throughout been chequered by sunshine and shadow. Or it may be that the first half of a life has been heaped up with all the blessings that can gladden the heart of man, and that the second half has been darkened by calamity after calamity, and that the day has moved to a painful or tragical close in storm and gloom. But in this common case also it is not impossible to reconcile the events with our faith in an educative discipline. We have enjoyed the benefits to the end that we may know the love which is in the heart of God, and learn to trust in God and in the future; we have been made to suffer to the end that we may acquire new graces of patience and sympathy, or break with some cherished sin, or cast down some idol, or that we may be led, in our helplessness or impoverishment, to seek our rest and sufficiency in God.

But while the main purpose of the educative plan of Providence is to purify, strengthen, and ennoble our characters, and to draw us more closely to God, there is another design which often appears to be clearly discernible, and that is that things befall us less for our own sakes than for the benefit of others. The purpose of our Lord's sufferings was declared to be twofold—on the one hand that He might Himself be made perfect through suffering, on the other hand that by His cross and passion He might become the Saviour of mankind. When St. Paul reflected on the divine meaning in the untoward and tormenting occurrences of his troubled life, he usually accounted for them as designed to purify his character, and throw him back on the grace of God; but sometimes also he explained them as designed to open up to him new opportunities of service, and to help on the work which had been given him to do as a missionary apostle. It was in the second way that our Lord explained the providential meaning of the calamity of the man born blind: whether or not his blindness made him a better man, it at least made an appeal to the sympathy of Christ and of Christlike men, and was the occasion of a manifestation of works worthy of God. We can at least see this meaning in human distress, He taught, that it gives others the privilege of helping to relieve it. There are numerous cases which may seem purposeless and even cruel, so far as the sufferer is concerned, but which have a use as a means of blessing to others. Many suffer as a warning to others not to break God's eternal laws. Some are delivered to death daily that others may live through their sacrifice. So one has known a woman tied for years to a bed of weakness and suffering, and it was prolonged after she herself might seem, humanly speaking, to have learned all the lessons of the Cross; but it did not seem useless in the retrospect when it appeared that in her period of tribulation she had hallowed the life of the home, taught her children the victorious power of Christian faith, and passed on through them to later generations a priceless spiritual inheritance.

The principles of the providential government thus set forth help to lighten the difficulty which is felt at an untimely death—the event which in these times has become so tragically common. Is it making too great a demand on our faith to ask us to believe that in many cases the providential reason is the same as that which is given for a boy passing from the school to the university, or leaving the home of his childhood to begin the work of life? The boy moves on to the new sphere because he had finished the preparation that belonged to the earlier stage of the school or the family; and it may well be that, from the divine point of view, those who pass early from the earthly sphere are, in many cases, those who have gained most of the advantage that was to be gained from the earthly discipline, and who have earned their promotion. If we believe in future probation we can think of the removal as bringing to others, if not promotion, at least new and better opportunities for the salvation of their souls. In other cases the explanation may rather be that they bless the world more by their going, or the manner of their going, than they would have done by a longer life.

It may be thought that I have spoken too confidently, if not presumptuously, of the hand of God in our individual lives. Many prefer to believe the fact of an enveloping Providence, but to speak of its aims and its ways as inscrutable. There are some modern homilies on Providence which show a great deal of faith, but not in Providence. They assume that what we owe to God is an orderly world in which it will go fairly well with us if we get to understand it, and adjust our lives accordingly; and as a substitute for a doctrine of Providence we are told to rely on the grace of God, which will be sufficient in temptation and trial, and which can make all things work together for our good. This is a profoundly true and a deeply needed gospel, but there is still a gospel of Providence which does something more than repeat the gospel of the grace of God, and gives us confidence in God as concerned even with the external happenings of our lives. The teaching of our Lord and His apostles, as has been said, proceeds on the footing that God knows and cares for each of His children, and that He surrounds them with a wise and holy plan in which even external things are ordered to the end of their greater goodness or usefulness. And of those providential aims many can find illustration and confirmation in their own past experience. It is remarkable how many of those who have done great things in the world—in the State as well as the Church—have been sustained by a childlike faith in a particular Providence. Many ordinary people, also, have reached a strong and deepening conviction that the outcome of their life has been the result of the interaction of a divine plan with the plans which they had framed for themselves. And as the years have passed they have thought less highly of their own wisdom, more highly of the wisdom of the Providence of God, and have also—though they may have been afflicted for their sins and visited with sufferings that seemed undeserved—been conscious that the general trend of their lives was directed towards their true good, and their greater usefulness, and that on the whole there was in their lot much manifestation of the calculated kindness of the Everlasting Father. Amen.

IV.

OUR MAKER.

"It is he that hath made us, and we are his."—PSALM c. 3 (R.V.).

ONE has known men and women of the older generation who uttered a creed, and declared their religion, simply by the reverent tone in which they spoke of God as "Our Maker." The title, as they spoke it expressed, not merely the fact that to God they owed their existence, but also that they were mindful of the great contrast between His majesty and their insignificance, and chiefly of their responsibility to Him as their Judge. The name is more rarely on our lips, but we may well meditate upon the fact that it is God who made us, and next upon the implications which are suggested in the less familiar but preferable reading, "and we are his."

I.

IT IS HE THAT MADE US.

We individual men and women are here, possessing the high dignity, and enjoying the rich privileges, of a human life on earth, and it is certain that we were not the authors of our own existence. When we consider how we came to be here, there are three stages in the process at which we are constrained to bow in adoration before God as our Maker.

1. There is, first, the stage of the origin of the individual soul. When we have learned all that can be taught by the physiologist, there remains the deeper problem of how the spiritual part of us came into being—that wonderful centre of our thoughts, feelings, and purposes to which we are constantly referring as " I," and which in reflective mood we call our soul. In regard to the genesis of the soul, or at least the commencement of its earthly life, various views have been held among philosophers and theologians. Following Plato, it was supposed by many thinkers of the ancient world, including some of the fathers of the Christian Church, that the soul of each individual enjoyed an earlier existence in the heavenly world, and that at a certain stage in the growth of the bodily organism which was being prepared for it the spiritual being was sent down from above, and lodged in its tenement of clay. The chief reasons given in support of this theory have been either that the mind contains ideas which it has brought from elsewhere, or that the inherited inequalities of the human lot are so glaring as to compel us to believe that we are here receiving the reward or the punishment due to our former deeds. It is, however, the impression of the great majority

that they recollect nothing whatever about a former
state, and it cannot be shown that the ideas of the
true, the good, and the beautiful which are found in
our minds are most plausibly explained as reminis-
cences.   It is true that we came "trailing clouds of
glory," but there are more convincing ways of account-
ing for the glory.   The inequalities of human life on
earth are usually explained by observing that we are
not only individuals whose lives reveal a plan of God,
but members of a race whose general life overflows
into ours under laws of its own.

In the Christian Church opinion has wavered
between two other views which are known in theology
as the traducian and the creationist hypotheses.   The
traducian theory is to the effect that the soul is transmitted from the parents, equally with the bodily
organism, and that we are as truly their children
after the spirit as after the flesh.   The strong point
in favour of this view is that mental and even moral
characteristics appear to be transmitted equally with
bodily qualities from parents to children.   There is,
however, a very real difficulty in seeing how spirit
can be subdivided, as if it were a thing with length,
breadth, and thickness, or, as an alternative, can be
developed out of a physical organism which to begin
with had nothing more in it than animal life.   We
seem thus to become materialists in our ideas about
ourselves, and if we do we have difficulty in opposing
the Materialism which finds no God in the universe.

The majority of Christian thinkers have accordingly preferred the theory that every new soul is brought into existence by an immediate act of the Creator. "He is perpetually creating souls out of nothing," it is held, "and creates each soul at the moment when the body which is destined for it enters really and properly on its inheritance of life." There is a difficulty, as has been indicated, in the facts of heredity, since it is not clear why God, if He creates each soul out of nothing, should imprint upon our soul the likeness of some of our ancestors, and still more is it a problem why God should be supposed so to create spiritual beings that they come into conscious existence with an endowment of evil tendencies. To the first of the objections it can be replied that God might, for wise purposes, create new souls which would have an affinity with those of the parents, and also that the influence of the inherited body upon the soul may be sufficient to bring about certain mental resemblances. As to the second, God does something in any case to allow sin to be perpetuated among men. At all events the objections are less serious than the difficulties of the traducian theory; and it remains the most probable view that the ever-repeated wonder of the appearance of another human soul is due to an immediate output of the life-giving energy of the Almighty, and that each of us is here because a few years ago God did a new thing in the realm of His creation, and brought into being the raw material of our unique personality.

2. We are also compelled to think of God as our

Maker when we ascend to the origin of the human race. Upon this subject the traditional ideas have been somewhat rudely shaken within the last hundred years. One of the great achievements of the nineteenth century, we are told, is its proof of the high antiquity of the human race. It was formerly supposed that man was created about 4000 years before the birth of Christ, and it is now said to be an assured result of historical and scientific research that civilised societies existed from 5000 to 10,000 years before our era, that before this mankind traversed long ages, in which they struggled upward to the threshold of civilisation, and that the infancy of our race lies in dim regions from which we are separated by 100,000 or even 250,000 years. Yet according to the scientific account, man's appearance on the planet is still comparatively recent as measured by geological standards. The series of the generations is not endless. We arrive at last, as we travel backward in the dark abyss of time, at a pair who were the progenitors of our human kind, and at the first man. How are we to conceive the manner of the making of the first man? There are several ways of thinking it out. There is the traditional conception that one day man leaped into existence and light, fully furnished in body, as well as in spirit, by the creative fiat of the Almighty. But even the mind which is predisposed to faith may feel that this is not how God does things in the realm of nature. It has been largely displaced by the purely evolutionary conception, according to which the first man was the offspring of two ape-like creatures, inherited from them a large stock of qualities which stamped them as brutes, but in addition diverged in the inexplicable way which sometimes happens in the course of nature, and varied so decidedly in the direction of reason and morality that it can be said that the dividing line was reached, and that for the first time a true man set foot upon the earth.   The objection to this is that man differs so widely from the brute, is so clearly a being of a different order, that we cannot easily suppose that the one passed into the other by a variation in degree of powers and capacities.   At the same time, even if the manner of man's making had been by gradual evolution, we could still believe as theists that he was the creature of God.   We should merely be asked to alter our views as to how God made man, and need not cease to believe that God made man.   The third view, which seems to me most probable, is that the first man sprang from parents of the animal world, but that at this particular stage God put forth the creative power which (as has been said) is probably still exerted at the beginning of the existence of each individual, and by the infusion of a human soul launched upon its career the species which was to manifest the image of God on the earth, and build upon the earth the Kingdom of God.   The writer of Genesis conceived of the first man as created by God first forming him out of the dust of the ground, and then breathing into his nostrils the breath of life; and this does not differ in principle from the theory that He laid hold of a pre-existing animal species, and endowed a member of it with a measure of His own spirit. Our intermediate view agrees with the intention of the scriptural narrative. It also seems more reasonable than the hypothesis that man evolved from the brutes through the operation of natural forces which gradually, and even by accidental variations, improved upon the animal till they had produced a man.

3. There is a sense in which God is our Maker, independently of our debt to Him in the matter of origins. It has been held by some philosophical thinkers that what we call the preservation of the world is of the nature of a continuous creation—that at every instant all finite things, including our souls and our bodies, drop back, so to speak, into nothingness, and that at every instant they are again brought into being by the power of the Almighty. This interesting speculation you need not be asked to accept. But even if God be not for ever re-creating, if He do nothing more than uphold us and all things in existence by the word of His power, if it be true, as it certainly is, that our strength would sink into inanition, and our souls pass out of existence should His sustaining hand be withdrawn from us, it means that for practical purposes God is for the third time our Creator, and that we are once more led to confess that it is He that made us, and not we ourselves.

II.

THE RESPONSIBILITY OF THE CREATOR.

If God is our Maker, and assuredly it is to Him and not to ourselves that we owe our existence and our continuance in existence, an important consequence follows. We have good reason to trust Him as the God who makes us the objects of His loving and efficient care, and upon whom we have an additional claim for the supply of our deepest and universal needs.

1. We are entitled to have confidence in our Maker, as one who will have a desire to the work of His hands. Every one takes a special interest in all that bears the impress of himself. Proverbially a parent has a peculiar fondness for his own children, which makes him sensitive to their needs, and also take a distinctive view of their defects; and this must hold, so far as may be without detriment to His veracity, of the Father of our spirits. It should be difficult, for example, for one who really believes that God is the Maker of the human race, to despair of the course of history and of human progress. In critical or pessimistic mood we may think that the history of mankind has been a failure, and may question if it has any interest save that of a tragic drama—if it is not even an irrational tale made up of sound and fury, which signifies nothing and will issue in nothing. But these ideas are the result of

exceptional experience and of short views. We may
be assured that the God who wrought so great a
wonder as the creation of the human race, and the
preparation of the earth to be its dwelling-place and
workshop, when He might as elsewhere have left this
corner of space unused and tenantless, would not have
brought them into existence had He not foreseen
that there would be a satisfactory conclusion to the
terrestrial enterprise, and that under His government
the human race would one day achieve results
which will be worthy of its outfit and redound to
the fuller glory of its Maker.

A similar consideration supports our faith in the
immortality of the individual soul. The mighty
Power which underlies and is at work in the universe
has wrought an astounding marvel in bringing us,
who once were not, into being, and in placing us
in possession of the Godlike faculties which think
His thoughts after Him, distinguish between good
and evil, and on the whole make and pursue plans
which are useful, noble and beautiful. And we may
well believe that the same Power did not intend to
mock us by delusive hopes founded on man's greatness,
and to put us to confusion by the catastrophe of
death, but that He purposes to preserve us amid
the shocks of change and dissolution, and to make
it possible to bring to a splendid consummation what
has been so wondrously begun in the strange and
glorious adventure of a human existence.

2. Again, when we reflect upon our debt to God as

our Maker, we may well feel the reasonableness of
the Christian belief that God is " a faithful Creator "
who added to His original benefactions by coming to
our succour as a Redeemer. Although the natural
endowments which we received from Him in Creation
were manifold and splendid, it is also true that there
are features of our lot with which man by his natural
powers is manifestly unable to cope. There are in
particular two afflicting and oppressing wants, of which
man has ever been conscious in moments of self-
knowledge. He was by nature incapable of rising to
the knowledge of God, and also of understanding his
own true character and destiny. And to ignorance
was added weakness. He was called upon to live
a life in conformity with high demands of duty, but
he was weighted by a nature in which there is as
much of the animal from whom he seems to be
descended as of the God whose image he bears, and
he was planted in a world in which it is usually
easier to fall back into the brute than to climb to
the height of the divine. Most credible, therefore,
seems the Christian belief, supported as the presumption is by heads of positive evidence, that God, taking
pity upon His creatures, enlightened their darkness
by the revelation which shined into the world in
Jesus Christ, and provided for our moral weakness
by the gift of the life and power from on high
for which we thank God as the gift of the Holy
Ghost.

III.

THE RESPONSIBILITY OF THE CREATURE.

A further consequence is that our Maker has a sovereign claim on our service. The God who created us has rights of property in us, and has a title to our obedience for the fulfilment of His commands and the execution of His purposes. "It is he that made us, and we are his"—to do His work. The same idea was repeated by St. Paul with a more distinct Christian background: "Ye are not your own; ye are bought with a price, therefore glorify God in your body, and in your spirit, which are God's." This principle is so familiar in our everyday life that it only needs to be understood to be accepted. We see the justice of the complaint made by the mouth of the prophet: "I have nourished and brought up children, and they have rebelled against me." When one man preserves the life of another, it is felt that a debt has been incurred which it will be impossible fully to pay. It is therefore clear that the God of Creation has a sovereign right to use us. We have absolutely no right to make our self-will, our private interests, our imagined well-being, the rule of our conduct. The insignificant self acts not only sinfully, but even ludicrously, when it sets up its own claims against the will of its Maker. It was the purpose, not only of the coming of Christ, but also of our coming into the world, which is described in the words of the Psalmist: "Lo, I come: in the volume of the book it is written of me, to do thy will, O God." But what are we to understand by this will of God which we, as His creatures, are here to do, and to assist in getting done? There are many short answers. It is another name for our duty. The will of God is revealed in the Scriptures. And again, the sum of the practical teaching of Scripture is that we should follow Christ. It is not, however, always easy to say what these standards require of us in detail, and most people accept as their rule the average practice of the circle in which they live, or the better tradition of their country and their church. We may get a fresh impression of the will of God by thinking of it in the two main aspects, which may be roughly distinguished as the will of God in the realm of nature and in the realm of grace.

First, there is a will of God, very definitely exemplified in the Old Testament, which is concerned with this world. It is undeniable that God has been, and is, largely concerned with interests which we commonly speak of as secular. The earth with its mountains, plains, and forests, its rivers, lakes, and seas, its stores of mineral wealth, its species of animals and birds, reptiles and insects, and all the utilities and beauties of the animate and the inanimate creation, came into existence because God found delight in planning them, and in translating His thoughts into facts.

Similarly, it was the doing of God that the human race was planted on this earth under conditions in which men had to earn their bread in the sweat of their brow, and to fight against want, disease, and death; and it was His manifest purpose that mankind should proceed to subdue the earth, to gain dominion over the animals, and to build up a great, rich, and complex civilisation. It must therefore be a fundamental duty of the individual man and woman to assist in carrying out this purpose of God as disclosed in the evolution of society and in the ordinary business of the world. It must be a cardinal duty to do something, whether by hand or by brain, which is of real value as a contribution to the everyday work of the world or at least as inspiration to those who do it, and it must be a serious dereliction of duty to pass through life without doing anything of this kind either to meet present needs or to help on future progress. What this observation leads to is that we ought to believe in the real sanctity of every vocation which has a necessary place in the subdivision of the labour of human societies. In its dread of seeming to encourage worldliness, the Church has done scant justice to the life of the men or women who, finding a calling which is in line with the great mundane purpose of the Creator, devote themselves to its duties with whole-hearted zeal and fidelity. Moreover, to be faithful in one's calling, provided only it be a useful calling, is to imitate Christ in one important particular, and it is also the most substantial way in which the average person can fulfil the command that we should show love to one another and bear one another's burdens.

There is also a will of God, known chiefly from the New Testament, which is connected with that economy of grace that bears witness to a faithful Creator. While God has a secular plan in regard to the human race in general, and has used up and will use up (if we may so speak) many generations in getting His plan set forward, He has at the same time pursued with individual souls the special end of a spiritual salvation. He has not overlooked the higher interests of those whom He required for the mundane tasks. He has not been like some slave-owner whose sole interest in his servants is that they are useful hands, and flings them aside when they are no longer serviceable for his business. The purpose which lies still nearer to His heart is to regard each individual as an end in himself, to lift him up to a richer life in union with Himself, and to treat the worn-out instruments of time as heirs of eternity. It is His will that here and now we should possess life eternal in the knowledge of Himself, and of Jesus Christ whom He has sent. "This is the will of God," says St. Paul, "even your sanctification." It is His will that we should rise by faith above the plane, not merely of the animal life, but of the self-centred human life, to that in which we are refashioned after the likeness of Christ by looking on His loveliness, and throwing our souls open to the renewing and enabling influences of the Holy Spirit. May we have grace to say, with some of this fulness of meaning, " God's will be done." Amen.

V

THE MAGNETISM OF THE CROSS.

"And I, if I be lifted up from the earth, will draw all men unto me."—JOHN xii. 32.

A MORE unlikely prophecy than this was never addressed to human ears. When the words were spoken it might well seem that the ministry of Jesus had ended in failure. The religious leaders of the Jews were enraged at Him, and were plotting His destruction. The common people, who at first had heard Him gladly, and sought to make Him a king, had become indifferent and even resentful; and only a handful of disciples continued loyal to His person and faithful to His cause. But in spite of the accumulating evidences of defeat, Jesus foretold that the issue would be a triumph more glorious and enduring than had entered into the boldest dreams of the disciples. He would be acknowledged as the Saviour and King, not of the Jews only, but of all mankind. More astounding still must it have seemed when Jesus spoke of the means by which the tide was to be turned, and victory plucked out of defeat. He had proclaimed His divine message, and it had fallen on deaf ears; He had performed mighty works, and they only credited Him with the help of Beelzebub. What greater thing would He do to change unbelief into faith, to transmute indifference into devotion and hatred into love? The reply was that the transformation would be brought about not by doing, but by suffering — by His voluntary surrender of Himself to the cruel death of the Cross at the hands of His enemies. We can only find it natural if the disciples sorrowfully reflected that this was indeed an unpromising way to reach the throne; and we can imagine how the Pharisees and Sadducees, in nowise abating their hatred, would laugh His prediction to scorn.

And yet it is matter of history that the prophecy has been accomplished both as to result and means. Jesus has drawn unto Himself, if not all men, at least representatives of all races and classes of the human family. The earth is girdled by a society, embracing men and women of every colour and tongue, of every rank and station, of every grade of intelligence, who are called by the name of Christ, who profess to believe His gospel, and who adore Him as their Saviour and Lord. And further it is evident that it was above all by reason of His sufferings and death that He took captive the heart, won the trust, and secured the allegiance of mankind. It is true that there are other factors which enter into the compelling power of Jesus Christ. It owes much to the spell of His teaching about God and man, salvation and duty—that teaching which in form was beautiful as the flowers of spring or the tints of the sunrise, in matter as high as the stars and as deep as the sea. Part of it also is due to the spell which is laid upon the soul by the character of Christ—in its unique union of heavenly majesty with a tenderness passing the love of woman. But it is above all as the Man of Sorrows, as the Crucified, that Jesus has been enthroned in believing hearts, and become the object of human love, gratitude and trust. In the churches which celebrate in ordered cycle the landmarks of our Lord's life, the year is felt to move to its climax in the commemoration of the great events of Passion Week. In our Presbyterian Church a substitute for this sacred season was formerly found in heart-searching preparation for the Sacrament of the Lord's Supper; and the solemn service itself has ever made the devout communicant to feel that he is thus brought into the Holy of Holies of his faith, where he experiences anew the truth of the Lord's prediction and promise that if He was lifted up from the earth He would draw all men unto Him.

Here, then, is one of the outstanding and most imposing of the facts of history—that Jesus Christ has brought into existence a spiritual society which links together nineteen centuries and holds the world in its embrace, and that He wields this power because He endured the Cross. Such a stupendous result can be explained only by the fact that the sufferings and death of Christ had a quality which stirs the deepest feelings of our common human nature, or which has a bearing upon the highest interests which belong to us as human beings. In reality the Cross of Christ has at least four different aspects, of which each makes a strong appeal to heart or mind, and which, in acting together, have invested it with a unique significance for the spiritual sense of mankind.

I.

THE TRAGEDY OF THE CROSS.

Beginning with its human aspect, we observe that the sufferings and death of Christ arrest our attention and claim our sympathy as the most tragical event recorded in history. The world has an open ear and a sensitive heart for a tale of overwhelming calamity that involves the innocent in shame and ruin; and no biography that was ever written, no train of events that was ever imagined, has approached in the elements of truest pathos to the record of the life and death of Jesus of Nazareth. Consider only the plain, central, and undisputed facts of the story as it is set forth in our Gospels. Upon this earth there appeared once a teacher who preached a gospel of divine and human love—who sought to persuade men to love the God who loved them in spite of their sins, and also to love one another, and to show their love by being kind, merciful, and forgiving. And as was His message, so was His life. He held

5

communion with the Father in a life of filial trust
and obedience and of stainless purity, while He spent
Himself and was spent in preaching the glad tidings
of the gospel to all, in saving outcast men and fallen
women from their degradation, and in assuaging,
whether by the power of His sympathy or of His
gifts of healing, the distress of many who had been
sorely stricken by disease or left poor and desolate
by the ravages of time and death. The world, with
its burdens of sin and sorrow, had need of Him;
there were reasons enough, one thinks, why it should
have welcomed Him; but as a fact it declared—and
this was the tragedy of it—that it could not even
make room for the holy and loving Jesus, and it rid
itself of Him as if His message were worse than
blasphemy, and His ministry one long-drawn crime.
Parties and classes which had their own standing
feuds made a truce for a season that they might
accomplish the destruction of Jesus. The Pharisees
who were regarded as men of God, the Sadducees who
were worldly and sceptical persons, the aristocracy and
the common people, the learned and the unlearned,
were united against Him by an extraordinary mixture
of motives, and to the end that He and His cause
might be the more effectually crushed, He was
doomed to suffer on the Cross the extremity of shame
and agony which was reserved for the worst of male-
factors. Little wonder, therefore, that when the
world came to know the true facts, its heart was
stirred to its depth with sympathy and remorse, and

that the story of the death of Christ was burned into its memory as a crime which is without parallel for a combination of self-deception and wickedness.

II.

THE DISCOVERY OF THE CROSS.

But next, the sufferings and death of Christ have taken their place in history as the occasion and means of a stupendous discovery. It is only a very partial account of the magnetism of the Cross to say that multitudes have thronged in imagination to Calvary to look upon the tragedy of the Crucifixion through the eyes of the disciples who watched afar off, and to feel the thrill, and shed a tear, of sympathy and sorrow. The Cross of Calvary also stands out memorably as the spot on which the human mind became assured of the certainty of the most sublime and important of all religious truths. In the same event which revealed the deceit and wickedness of the human heart was found the revelation of the truth that God is love. The world had before this some conception of the divine greatness and majesty. That God was inconceivably great and infinitely wise was written upon the face of nature. That He was just and benevolent was also disclosed in the realm of nature, and His righteousness had been confidently proclaimed by the great prophets of the Old Testament who had been given the insight to interpret His works, and to

expound His acts of judgment.   But there was still
room for a haunting and oppressive doubt in the
world's heart.   God was just, but perhaps only just
—paying to the righteous their due, but no more,
recompensing the wicked in strict retribution unto
the uttermost farthing of their merited punishment.
He might be benevolent, but only in the general sense
of lavishing gifts that it cost Him nothing to dispense.
Was there reason to believe that in the Divine Being
mercy met with justice, and that He loved man with
a love of the kind that is equal to self-sacrifice?
The answer to this question was given, not merely by
the word of a prophet, but in and through a life; and
the response was that the death of Christ completed and
sealed the revelation that in God is a love which is strong
and unquenchable, which attests itself in suffering and
humiliation, and which recompenses evil with good.

But how did the death of Christ serve as a revelation and confirmation of the love of God?   In two
ways.   In the first place, as is expressed in many
passages in the New Testament, we can read the
mind and heart of a giver from the nature of his
gifts ; and when we consider the gift of God to the
world in Jesus Christ, holy, meek, compassionate, who
lived to do good, and who suffered death in the discharge of His vocation of loving service, we can
believe that that stainless and self-sacrificing life was
the gift of a God who was holy as Jesus was holy,
and who loved man as Jesus loved.   This argument of
faith is of the same kind as that which might be framed

by some tribe of degraded savages who, coming to understand the work and to revere the personality of a devoted
missionary, would draw a trustworthy inference as to
the character and aims of the society which had sent
him to minister to them, or as to the mind of a saintly
mother who had dedicated her son to their service.

But besides the argument from the nature of the
gift, it is an element of the faith of Christendom not
only that God was witnessed to by Christ, but that
God was in Christ—that He who suffered and died
upon the cross was in a unique sense divine.   What,
then, is meant by affirming that the crucified Christ
was divine?   Nothing is more striking than the
pertinacity with which the Church, in all its branches,
cleaves to the article of the divinity of Christ.   Men
cling passionately to a part of the doctrine even when
they feel unable to affirm the whole of the doctrine
which is embodied in the Catholic faith.   There is
one school which calls Christ divine because in His
person and life He revealed the character of God, and
because in His influence upon men's souls He does
the work of God.   In Him, they say, we saw manifested the qualities that are highest in God—a power
that had mastery over the world, a superhuman
wisdom, a perfectly holy will and an infinitely loving
heart ; by Him, moreover, the highest work of God
continues to be performed in the renewal and sanctification of human souls ; and we are constrained to
address to Him who is supremely Godlike in Himself and in His work the confession of Thomas,

"My Lord and my God." Those who hold the divinity of Christ in this limited sense of His Godlikeness—calling Him God because of His sinless perfection, His tireless holy love, and the power of His grace—have seized a part of the truth, which is also a profoundly important truth, and which supplies a spiritual provision by which a soul is helped to live. But while the faith in the Godlikeness and godlike work of Christ may help us to grope our way through the darkness, and to struggle against the difficulties and temptations of the world, it is in the power of a fuller conception of the meaning of Christ's divinity that the Church has done its enduring work, and that the saints have lived and died. For them the divinity of Christ has meant that He who was born in Bethlehem and crucified on Calvary was not merely a manifestation in time of godlike qualities and purpose, but eternally God—"One Lord Jesus Christ, the only-begotten Son of God, begotten of the Father before all worlds, God of God, Light of Light, very God of very God, begotten not made, being of one substance with the Father, by whom all things were made: who for us men and for our salvation came down from heaven."

III.

THE MYSTERY OF THE CROSS.

Yet again, there is a fascination in mystery; and an element of mystery enters into the magnetism of the

Cross. There are problems connected with the death of Christ—with the reason why it was necessary for the Saviour of the world to die—that have fascinated the most earnest and profound minds throughout the Christian centuries. We feel, moreover, that there were aspects of the Saviour's sufferings with which we may not intermeddle — experiences which we cannot fathom. We cannot gauge or estimate the agony that must have been endured by His pure and stainless spirit in breathing the atmosphere of wickedness and crime, nor can we understand the anguish that He felt when He prayed that the cup might pass from Him, or that wrung from Him the awful cry, "My God, my God, why hast thou forsaken me?" There lie mysteries toward which the curiosity of the devout mind is irresistibly drawn, and which are also a hall-mark of truth, for as has been well said, "A religion without its mysteries is like a temple without a God."

IV.

THE EFFICACY OF THE CROSS.

There is another feature of the Cross of Christ which has exercised a still more potent influence than its deep pathos, its thrilling discovery, and its halo of mystery, and that is that it has been felt to possess a peculiar efficacy—to be the means by which unique benefits have been brought within the reach of sin-stricken and sorrow-laden souls. It is natural that that should evoke our deepest interest which promises to give us deliverance from evil, and to increase our well-being; and it is pardonable as well as natural that mankind should have been deeply impressed by an event which contains the promise of removing or lightening the heavy burdens which make up so large a part of the spiritual distress of the human lot. Let us touch briefly on two main aspects of the efficacy of the Cross of Christ as it has been experienced in relation to sin and sorrow.

1. In the first place, the death of Christ is bound up with the necessary and comforting gospel of the forgiveness of sins. It is said that men of our generation no longer have the same sensitive consciousness, which was distinctive of the older piety, of the guilt of sin, and of the need of pardon; and it is undoubted that there are many influences at work which tend to weaken the sense of responsibility and of blame-worthiness; but I believe that deep down in the being of all of us there goes on an ineradicable work of conscience which brings home to us in our times of solemn self-communing that our souls are stained with sin, that the story of our lives is full of transgression and shortcoming, that we have griev-ously offended against a just and holy God, and that the deepest need of our souls is the assurance of His mercy and forgiveness. And in the hour when we thus realise our unworthiness, not only do we say, " God be merciful to me a sinner," but we instinctively

add, "for Christ's sake." We feel that we can more confidently trust in the pardoning love of God when we not merely plead our penitence and the grace of the Heavenly Father, and His own name's sake, but when we link our unworthiness to that of the altogether worthy, and urge the merits of Him whose soul was without spot or blemish, and who was obedient unto death in the sacrifice of Calvary.

2. In the second place, it is evident that a new power comes into the life, in the battle with temptation, and in the bearing of our burdens of sorrow, through the gospel of the tempted and sorrowing Saviour. It is a trite observation that only those can truly sympathise with trial and grief who have themselves been shaken and harrowed by a similar experience. We are apt to discount the advice and the consolation of those who have not themselves been tested in the furnace.   And there is nothing in the Christian gospel, save its message of a gracious forgiveness, which has so powerfully appealed to the heart of men as the truth that God can sympathise with us in our trials, because the worst which can befall in human experience has been gathered up into the life of God in the experience of the Son of God. We may find it difficult to formulate precisely in our own thoughts what is meant by the presence of Christ at God's right hand, and the ministries of His Heavenly Priesthood ; but the practical significance is that we can trust God for a human heart as well as for infinite wisdom and power, that we can be assured that we

are present to His mind in every detail of our burdens
of sorrow and sin, that He understands with the
sympathetic understanding of one who knows all the
fierceness of our temptations and all the heaviness
of our sorrows, and also that the way of the Cross,
when appointed by God and followed in trust and
submission, is the way to the everlasting crown.

In conclusion, let us ask how we are to make our
own the benefits of our Lord's passion? With what
motive do we stand and gaze before the Cross, and
what response should it evoke? When we study the
hymns which have as their theme the sufferings and
death of Christ, we find that they express a variety
of moods, and reflect different attitudes of soul. In
some passages the prevailing note is one of sympathy,
even of compassion, for the Man of Sorrows, which
invites us to mingle our tears with the agonies and
cries of the Crucified.

> "Who upon that Sufferer gazing,
>   Bowed in sorrow so amazing,
>   Would not with His mother mourn?"

And again,

> "Have we no tears to shed for Him,
>   While soldiers scoff and Jews deride?
>   Ah! look how patiently He hangs!
>   Jesus, our Lord, is crucified."

This mood is more distinctive of Roman Catholic
than of Protestant piety, and may merely have a senti-

mental value—of the same kind as the feelings which are stirred within us at the contemplation of similar tragedies in the life of nations or individuals. The sentimental view becomes religious only when we connect the sins which nailed Jesus to the tree with the sins of our own hearts and lives that spring from the same root, and when our pity passes into penitence—as indeed it usually does in the hymns with this vein:

> "O break, O break, hard heart of mine,
> Thy weak self-love and guilty pride
> His Pilate and His Judas were :
> Jesus, our Lord, is crucified."

There is, again, the attitude of obedience and docility, in which we think of Christ as the example in wrestling and agony which

> ". . . in the garden secretly,
> And on the cross on high,
> Should teach His brethren, and inspire
> To suffer and to die."

The most edifying mood is that which voices itself in an appropriating and a triumphant faith:

> "How came the everlasting Son,
> The Lord of Life, to die?
> Why didst Thou meet the tempter's power,
> Why, Jesus, in Thy dying hour
> Endure such agony?
>
> To save us by Thy precious blood,
> To make us one in Thee,
> That ours might be Thy perfect life,
> Thy thorny crown, Thy cross, Thy strife,
> And ours the victory."   Amen.

VI.

FREE GRACE.

"I have given you a land for which ye did not labour, and cities which ye built not, and ye dwell in them; of the vineyards and oliveyards which ye planted not do ye eat. Now therefore . . ."—JOSHUA xxiv. 13, 14.

IF we count up the most valuable things which we own and enjoy, we find that about almost all of them two remarks can be made: one that they do not cost us much, the other that at some time and to some other persons they cost a heavy price. In the realm of religion these things are spoken of under the names of free grace and vicarious sacrifice, but it is more rarely noticed that they are traceable to a large extent in the realm of nature as well as in the realm of grace. · Bishop Butler wrote a famous book in which he worked out an analogy between the system of the natural world and the scheme of the Gospel and nowhere is the analogy more striking than in the wide range of the principles which we have mentioned. They are the essence of spiritual laws which run through the whole natural world.

I.

THE REIGN OF GRACE.

Our text supplies an illustration which, though not on a high ethical level, at least brings out the nature of grace with its background of sacrifice. The writer is recalling the conquest by the children of Israel of the land of Canaan. It was an old land which for centuries had been the seat of an industrious and fairly civilised people. The earlier inhabitants had replenished the earth and subdued it; they had made it a country of teeming flocks and fertile fields; they had their workshops and their trade; they had their towns and cities stored with the treasures of the past and with their own accumulated wealth. Then the tempest burst upon their heads. The Hebrews, a people in arms, came up out of the desert, crossed the Jordan, defeated the Canaanites in battle, and served themselves heirs to their valuable and hard-won possessions. The moral aspect of the situation did not trouble the Jewish conscience, or was disposed of by the reflection that they had an ancient title to the land in which their fathers had once sojourned, and above all that it was a gift to them from the God whom they served, and who had crowned their arms with victory. It was not felt that there was any occasion to pity the old inhabitants whose industry and skill had made Canaan so rich a prize: the only feeling was gratitude at the

easy terms on which their possessions had passed into
the hands of the nomads from the desert.   And the
feeling was put in words which were yet to fit far grander
themes : " The Lord hath given you a land for which
ye did not labour, and cities which ye built not, and
ye dwell in them; of the vineyards and oliveyards
which ye planted not do ye eat."

2. We observe next that the event of which
Joshua spoke is repeated in its main features in the
relations of the successive generations of mankind.
It takes place, not only in the violent way of conquest and spoliation, but also in the peaceful way in
which, in the course of nature, one generation labours
and those which follow enter into its labours.   When
we look around us in a rich old land like our own,
we see it heaped up with material wealth which has
been gratuitously received by the living as their inheritance from the far larger population that has now
its earthly lodging in the crowded graveyards.   There
are the roads and the railways, the cultivated fields,
the villages and towns with the buildings that stand
for centuries; in addition, the vast accumulation of
knowledge and experience, of inventions and skill,
which constitute the foundation and the machinery
of material well-being—a stupendous creation in
which was embodied infinitely more than we can
measure or imagine of human planning and toil and
sweat, and even of the lives and the souls of men.
And while it is true that this patrimony is not
administered on terms of pure grace, since a large part

of the material wealth requires to be reproduced in each
generation, it is still true that it was owing to the
bequest from our ancestors that we found ourselves in
civilisation and not in savagery, and it has been
handed on without money and without price by those
to whom we can now make no acknowledgment and
offer no return.

3. Still more conspicuously are the principles of
sacrifice and grace revealed in the conditions on which
a people holds its higher or spiritual possessions.
The matter might even be illustrated from the inheritance of language and literature. A great language, like our own, is one of the wonders of the
world; every new word, every phrase that lived, was
once an original and happy stroke of genius; the
language as a whole is a consummate work of genius;
and when our minds developed we found it lying
ready-made for all uses, great and small, of which our
powers were capable. The literature which the world
agrees to call great had a heavier original cost.
Carlyle was fond of repeating that there was never
a man with the prophet's insight who had not eaten
his bread in sorrow; and it is no accident that the
most precious portions of our Bible come from the
prophets who spoke for or to a nation when it was
being hammered on the anvil or purified in the
furnace, and from Christ and His disciples when they
were looking forward to or looking back upon the
Cross. The golden ages in the history of literature
seem all to have had a background, if not of tragedy,

at least of costly enterprise and perilous conflict. Of the poets it has been said, with large measure of truth, that they "learned in suffering what they taught in song." And the terms are easy on which we receive the gift that comes to us stained with tears and blood: the treasures are available for us in cheap editions and free libraries, and they can be appropriated by the poorest as the result of a free education.

4. The same observations are made when we go through the list of the rights and privileges which make up the spiritual patrimony of our people. National independence was counted a thing of such value by our ancestors that, in order to maintain it, they paid heavy toll through many centuries of such wealth as they possessed, and of the richest of their blood. We have our social and political liberties—freedom of migration, freedom of thought, freedom of speech, a voice in controlling and guiding the destinies of our country; and such things were once won in rebellions and civil war. We have our religious liberties, of which the chiefest is that men have been delivered from a spiritual tyranny, that they choose their own creed, and worship God, according to their conscience; and the reason of it is that this land once produced men who deemed that nothing else was so much worth living for, and that such liberty was also worth dying for if it could not be otherwise purchased. And in this region we are especially impressed by the disproportion between the original sacrifice and the terms on which the benefits are transmitted. Very

light are the succession duties which are exacted from the heirs of the spiritual patrimony. We have enjoyed our rights of conscience and kindred liberties as freely as the air we breathed, and can practically say that, what once cost others everything, we have taken over for nothing.

5. Finally, the argument carries us into the inmost sanctuary of our religion. The chief difference is what we might have expected—that as the blessings here spoken of are the greatest conceivable, so the sacrifice which they demanded was the costliest conceivable, while the conditions of possession are described in terms of unqualified free grace. The blessings are the greatest that the heart can conceive: the forgiveness of sins, the friendship of God, the presence in the soul of the Holy Ghost, the Lord and giver of life, victory over the world with all its sin and evil, and the title to a life to come with an exceeding weight of glory. And the doctrine of the gospel is that the ground and foundation of the sovereign blessings is an unparalleled sacrifice. It is declared that they rest on a sacrifice which was unique—in respect of the dignity of the Sufferer, of the purity and blamelessness of the victim, of His obedience unto death under the most cruel agonies both of body and of soul. It was also unique, as we beheve with the apostles, in that it was a sacrifice which carried the Cross even into the life of God, who spared not His own Son, but gave Him up to die for sinners of mankind.

Not less is it distinctive of the Christian gospel

6

that it declares that the blessings which were purchased by an unexampled sacrifice are dispensed on
terms of unsurpassable magnanimity. The heart of
the gospel is that we may claim forgiveness, and all
other blessings which follow in its train, by that act of
childlike trust in the mercy of God which bears the
name of faith. The essence of the Christian religion
is that those who believe are comforted by God's forgiveness to the end that they may become good, not
that they are commanded to become good in the hope
of meriting the favour of God. " By grace ye are
saved through faith, and that not of yourselves, it is
the gift of God."

I do not think that this gratuitous character of the
Christian salvation is at all generally understood.
Perhaps a majority of Christians have always thought,
like the Jewish Christians whom St. Paul addressed in
the Epistle to the Galatians, that they are not under
grace but under the law—that they are in the same
position spiritually in which a man finds himself in
this world who, being poor, sets out to make a fortune,
or being ignorant sets out to acquire learning, and
that they have to achieve their purpose by labour,
perseverance and desert. But this is precisely the
view which Paul declared to be the chiefest misunder-
standing. The blessings of the gospel, he reiterated,
are not the reward of achievements, but gifts. He had
found that in his own experience God dealt with him
on terms of pure grace; and he also found that the
gospel of grace was in harmony with the character of

God and with the needs of men. God was too great, he felt, not to do things in the grandest way. On the other hand, man was too weak in his sin-bound nature to hope to be able to accomplish anything that would merit the favour of God. The doctrine of free grace can be readily misunderstood and easily abused, and, as Hooker says, may be "counted folly or frenzy or fury." But with Hooker many have added in all ages : "It is our wisdom and our comfort; we care for no knowledge in the world but this, that God hath made Himself the sin of men, and that men are made the righteousness of God."

II.

THE COROLLARIES.

Clearly, then, the principles of vicarious sacrifice and free grace permeate and enrich the whole of the higher domains of human life. Let us next consider some of the implications and consequences of this striking condition of the human lot.

1. In the first place, we are entitled to put forward a claim for those who made the vicarious sacrifices. In tracing the principle of grace as rooted in sacrifice we may often be oppressed by the feeling that there runs through such a system a strain of injustice. Is it just that some should endure the labours and the sufferings, and that others should enter into their labours and reap the fruits? When Joshua rejoices in the spoils of his conquest, we are provoked to sym-

pathise with the despoiled Canaanites rather than
with the children of Israel, and we may have the
same feeling when we think of the more valuable
possessions which have been shown to illustrate the
reign of grace. Why should one generation suffer
that another may rejoice? Why should one labour
and travail in spirit, and another make its home in its
cities, and gather the harvest of its vineyards and
its oliveyards? Why should the martyr go to the
scaffold and die that lesser souls may have the free gift
of their liberties?

What have we to say to this apparent injustice
which clings to the system of vicarious suffering?
Some think that there is a sufficient explanation and
justification in what is called the solidarity of the
human race. They say that we must look upon
mankind, or upon the nation, as a whole, and that it is
a sufficient reward for those who have paid the price,
that their country, or it may be the world, will be
the better and the richer for their offering. To many,
however, of our serious thinkers, it has seemed that the
difficulty can be satisfactorily met only if we believe
in individual immortality, and hold that a Divine
Judge will one day render to every man according to
his works. It does not consist with our divinely implanted conception of justice that those who sowed
should be denied a hand in the reaping. It is an un-
welcome thought, not only to Christian faith, but to
a mind which believes in a rational government of the
world, that nothing remains of vanished peoples which

toiled and suffered for human progress save mounds of dust and ashes, or that heroes and martyrs who died in some noble cause should themselves have no knowledge of or conscious share in the blessings which they won for others at such a price. It is true that many of those who have done most for the world have asked nothing for themselves, but have been content to do the duty which was plain to them, and to leave the reward, if such there be, to the discretion of a higher Power. But we are entitled to believe that the best results of human history are gathered up in their essence in the souls which live on in the unseen world of spirits, and that it lies in the will and in the power of God, not only to save them alive, but to give them, as was written of the suffering servant, to see of the travail of their soul and to be satisfied therewith.

2. The practical corollary is that those who have lived under the reign of free grace should themselves be willing, if their turn comes, to take over the part of vicarious sacrifice. As a fact, this call has been made upon our generation, and we have seen with our own eyes a sudden and startling transformation in the rôle of our people. Formerly our life seemed to be built up mainly of inherited privilege, and as in a night it has taken on the character of vicarious suffering. The sacrifice is still too near and too overwhelming for us fully to realise its magnitude—to realise what it means, even on the material side, that wealth measured by thousands of millions should be used up

in a work of destruction ; still more what it means for the life of the nation that three millions of men should be taken from their peaceful avocations and flung into the furnace of the fighting line, that our land should be radically impoverished by so many of the best of our people being cut down in their youth or in their prime, and that with our depleted powers we should have to look forward to carry on the most crushing burdens, and to solve the hardest problems, with which the nation has ever been confronted in its history. There is no evidence, but the contrary, that our people have grudged the sacrifice. Had we only been contending for a selfish advantage, the nation would have been rent in twain, and the explanation of its unanimity is the creditable one that it feels that, besides fighting in its own defence, it had to prove faithful to a great trust in the continuance of its historical mission of service, in the championship of wronged nations, and in the vindication of the moral law as having some bearing on the relations one with another of the nations of the earth. Whatever the other consequences may prove to be, the great sacrifice has certainly raised the nation as a whole in the scale of moral dignity. It can feel itself to be no longer a pauper generation living on the bounty of bygone benefactors, but a martyr generation which has itself been called on to pay the customary cost of all great things in toil and tears and blood, and which has thus qualified to hand on a great inheritance to the generations which are to come.

In the sphere of personal religion the obligation is

similar: "Freely ye have received, freely give."
From the days of St. Paul the gospel of free grace
has been objected to on the ground that if God's chief
blessings of pardon and eternal life are looked on as
gifts, which need only be claimed by faith, the easy
religion will bear fruit in an easy morality. But
Paul did not think so. His expectation, supported
by his own experience, was that when the soul is in
earnest, and throws all its energy into the act of
appropriating faith, and knows the value of what it
has claimed and received, it will be constrained by
gratitude to make an appropriate return in a holy
and beneficent life. In view of the overwhelming
mercies of God, the service of God in all good works
should seem the reasonable, even the inevitable, service.
It was in the same way that the Reformers argued
when it was objected that if there was no merit in
good works, men would become careless in their lives,
and in particular would cease to care for the poor.
They replied that they reckoned on the gratitude of
those who believe that Christ died for them, and that
God has graciously pardoned them in their unworthiness. It was a sublime confidence which they showed,
and it has not been very impressively justified except in
the lives of the saints. But even we average Christians
should be able to realise the force of the appeal that the
God to whom we owe all, and to whom we owe our
best in Christ, has in the gospel put us on our honour
to live soberly and righteously in the world, and to
love one another as God has loved us. Amen.

VII.

REPENTANCE.

" Repent ye."—MARK i. 15.

IN a Scottish parish in the olden days, when the Communion was an annual event, it was preceded by a season of solemn preparation which included a discipline of self-examination, fasting, and humiliation before God. The greater frequency of our celebrations, apart from deeper causes, has reduced the preparatory exercises to a shadowy form, but we may at least find occasion for a meditation on the special duty which the Communion season was wont to urge imperiously on mind and conscience. This is the duty of Repentance.

Repentance is everywhere insisted on in the Scriptures as one of the fundamental obligations of true religion. The preaching of the Old Testament prophets was essentially a call to repentance. When our Lord invited men to enter the Kingdom of God He said that the conditions of entrance were faith and repentance. There was a violent controversy between Roman Catholics and Protestants as to whether

Penance was to be reckoned a sacrament, but they were at least agreed that repentance is necessary to the Christian character and to the attainment of eternal salvation. The general idea of repentance was expressed in the Old Testament as a turning from sin to God and righteousness. In the New Testament the word usually employed denotes a change of heart, which makes a man to see things in a new light, feel new affections, and act in accordance with new principles of conduct. And this experience may be either total or partial. It may be so radical and thoroughgoing as to transform the character and alter the general outlook and attitude of the soul; or it may be a partial repentance which is called for by a particular sinful act or evil habit.

I.

THE GENERAL REPENTANCE.

We begin with the wider meaning of repentance as a change of heart which involves, not merely the abandonment of particular sins, but the hatred of sin as sin. "There is but one repentance in a man's whole life," says Jeremy Taylor, "in the strict and proper sense; and it takes place when our whole life is changed from the state of sin and death to the life of grace and the possession of Christ." It is in the same way that repentance is understood in the Shorter Catechism, where it is defined as " a saving grace, whereby a sinner out of a true sense of his sin, and apprehension of the mercy of God in Christ, doth with grief and hatred of his sin turn from it unto God, with full purpose of and endeavour after new obedience." The distinction between those who have thus broken in principle with sin and those who have repented not was never more impressively drawn than in a passage of the old Scots Confession which was penned by John Knox: "For how soon that ever the spirit of the Lord Jesus takes possession of the heart of any man, so soon does He regenerate and renew the same man, so that he begins to hate that which before he loved, and begins to love that which before he hated; and from thence comes that continual battle which is betwixt the flesh and the spirit in God's children. This battle have not the carnal men who, destitute of God's spirit, lust for things pleasing and delectable unto the self, and do follow and obey sin with greediness, and without repentance, even as the Devil and their corrupt lusts do prick them. But the sons of God (as before said) do fight against sin, do sob and mourn when they perceive themselves tempted to iniquity, and if they fall they rise again with earnest and unfeigned repentance. And these things they do, not by their own power, but the power of the Lord Jesus (without whom they can do nothing) worketh in them all that is good."

It may, indeed, be thought that the difference of the two classes of the repentant and the unrepentant is not now so clearly marked as it appeared to be to John Knox. Christian people do not seem to have the same sense as formerly of sin as a penetrative and leavening principle, hateful and loathsome in all its forms, with which they are at war; and on the other hand those whom the Reformer described as carnal have appropriated in greater or lesser measure the guidance and the rebukes of the Christian conscience. At the same time it is an undeniable fact of experience that that fundamental alteration of character does take place which the Catechism calls Repentance unto Life; and it is equally undeniable that there are many who feel that the one thing needful for them is a radical change of heart and purpose. There are not a few who have a humiliating and galling sense that their character, and the general tenor and spirit of their life, are unsatisfactory; that they are in bondage, if not to the lusts of the flesh, at least to the tyranny of the world, and the still greater tyranny of their self-love; and who feel that, if they are to attain to true tranquillity of soul, and to rejoice in their life, they must be delivered from the thraldom, and caught up into a world of more spiritual and unselfish aims. The difficulty is that, while nothing seems so well worth having as a change of heart, nothing also seems more difficult to procure. The testimony of those who have experienced this shifting of the centre of their personality is that at bottom it was not an act of their own, but a work of the Spirit of God—that it was not by their might, nor

by their power, but by the Spirit of the Lord of
Hosts. By grace they were saved through faith,
and that not of themselves, it was the gift of God.
It also appears from numerous biographies, of which
St. Paul's is typical, that many who have been lifted
up to the plane of spiritual life have undergone the
experience when they were not seeking it, not
praying for it, perhaps even fighting against it.
But, on the other hand, numerous cases have also
been chronicled where the deliverance has followed
upon a resolute determination to rise into the truer
and purer life. The earliest recorded example is
that of Jacob, who wrestled with the angel and cried,
"I will not let thee go, unless thou bless me." Our
Lord recognised it when He said that the Kingdom
of Heaven suffereth violence and the violent take it
by force. We find the same experience repeated in
records of the religious life of later times, and that
not merely in the school which has less of the
evangelical spirit. Resolution, as might have been
expected, is a prominent feature in the account of
his conversion given by Kingsley. "Last night,"
he wrote, "my birth-night, I spent an hour upon
the seashore, forming determinations which are to
effect my destiny through time and through eternity.
. . . I am saved, from pride, from scepticism, from
sensuality, restored ￼to my God." But the sense of
resolute self-determination was equally emphatic in
the record of Finney the American revivalist, who
relates of his conversion—"the question seemed to be,

will you accept Christ now, to-day. I said, I will accept Him, or die in the attempt." No doubt beneath and behind such resolutions there is an influence of the Spirit of God, but it is well to remember that God may make the Kingdom of God approach us in the light of a task to be achieved rather than of a gift to be received.

II.

REPENTANCE IN DETAIL.

From the subject of the general repentance, which practically coincides with conversion, we pass to the consideration of the duty of repenting of specific sins. "Men ought not to content themselves," as is wisely said in the Westminster Confession, "with a general repentance, but it is every man's duty to endeavour to repent of his particular sins particularly." We first note the two main classes of these particular sins, and thereafter we shall consider the parts or stages of a genuine repentance in regard to them.

1. One class of particular sins includes acts of wrong-doing of a somewhat heinous kind. The extreme example is a crime. I do not suppose that there is any one addressed by this sermon whose memory is haunted by some dark crime, in the fashion which has furnished so much fascinating material to the dramatist and the novelist, and who has been pursued for years by the terrors of an avenging conscience.

It is, however, practically certain that some have been at least entangled in vice, and have been degraded by surrender to the lusts of the flesh. It is still more certain that if an inquiry were instituted into our past lives, many could call to mind injuries to their neighbour which were somewhat heinous sins either against justice or against love. It would be a very useful exercise for the average man of a Sunday to run over his life with a view to make a list of all to whom he had ever done a real wrong, and if the inquiry were prosecuted with candour he would probably be surprised at the length of the accusing list. There are also sins against love which ought to be recalled; and women as well as men may be somewhat confidently invited to consider the names of those whom they alienated or made enemies of by unkind or unjust treatment, and who passed out of their lives with indifference or hatred in their hearts.

The second class of sins which call for particular repentance consist of evil habits. The grosser forms are exemplified by the habits of drunkenness and of the impure life, but there are many others which, though less disreputable, are in the sight of God hardly less of a disfigurement of the soul. There is the deep-seated and all-pervasive habit of making self the point of view from which everything is regarded, and the pivot round which most actions revolve. There is the habit of vanity—apt to grow with the years—which is the root of envy, jealousy, and meanness, as well as a source of constant

disturbance of mind. There are the habits of despond-
ency, of a sullen or irritable temper, of a censorious
judgment and a bitter tongue. There is the habit of
shunning hardship and opposition, and following the
line of greatest ease and comfort. The truth is that our
character is, and tends ever more to become, a bundle
of moral habitudes, and there are few of us who
are not able, in moods of candour and self-insight,
to draw up against ourselves a somewhat humbling
indictment.

2. Of the wicked deed, then, and the evil habit,
men are called to repent particularly, and we have
next to distinguish the chief parts or stages of a
genuine repentance in regard to them. The first stage
is heartfelt sorrow for the sin. This may be expressed
with varying degrees of emphasis—from the flood of
tears and the sackcloth and ashes of the Oriental
penitent, to the inward pang and the bowed head of
the restrained Western soul. And here it is important
to distinguish two different kinds of sorrow, which are
of very unequal spiritual value. One, called in
theology attrition, is sorrow for the suffering or loss
which a sin may have wrought, and the shame it may
have entailed—as when a criminal or a drunkard is
merely angry with himself for having played the fool,
or a selfish man upbraids himself for his short-
sightedness in having driven love out of his life, and
prepared for himself a friendless and cheerless old age.
This is the sorrow of the world which, in St. Paul's
phrase, "worketh death." Instead of exercising a healing

and reconciling influence, it may only plunge the soul into deeper depths of gloom and bitterness, and drive it to a greater distance from God. The true contrition is that in which a sin is felt, apart from its consequences for the sinner, to be hateful because of its wickedness, and above all, because it is an offence against the goodness and the long-suffering of a holy God. It was genuine contrition when the Psalmist said, "Against thee, thee only have I sinned," and when the prodigal purposed to return and say, "Father, I have sinned against heaven and in thy sight." It was in contrition that Peter went out and wept bitterly. This is the sorrow which needeth not to be repented of—which brings the sinner face to face with God, bespeaks His forgiveness, and is the earnest of his reformation.

The second part of a true repentance is confession of the sinful deed or habit. It is our duty to confess our sins to God—and that not merely in the general terms used in public prayer when we declare ourselves to be miserable sinners, but by recalling in our private prayers any grave actual sins of which our consciences accuse us, and making mention of the evil habits which have established a tyranny in our lives. The twofold use of this is obvious—it is promised that if we confess our sins, God is faithful and just to forgive us our sins; and on the other hand it is impossible for a sincere and self-respecting man or woman to make such confession to God without being impelled to make fresh endeavours after deliverance and victory. It is a controversial

question how far, and in what way, the confession of
our sins to God should be supplemented by confession
to a fellow-man. The Roman Catholic Church
requires of its faithful members that they shall
confess to a priest, at least once a year, all deadly
sins, and recommends the confession in addition of
their venial sins. To us the system of the Confessional
is repugnant on grounds of religious principle and of
racial temperament, nor are we much impressed by the
observed results. But it does not follow, because the
Roman Catholic Church has worked it out badly,
that there is nothing in the principle on which its
Confessional is founded. General and compulsory
confession is likely either to do harm or to degenerate
into a mere form, and yet there may be a real place
and use for occasional and voluntary confession as a
means of relief for burdened consciences. There is
many a heart which has been bruised and broken by
remorse that would have found balm and comfort by
pouring its confidences into a sympathetic ear. There
is a powerful natural instinct which impels us to seek
a confidant in every deep trouble of the soul, and it is
doubtful if for this our Church has made sufficient
provision. A minister is not an official confessor, but
more use might be voluntarily made of his guidance,
than is usual in Scotland, by those whose consciences
torment them because of some bygone transgressions
or challenge them to renew the apparently hopeless
struggle with a bad habit. It seems to be as natural
and necessary that there should be spiritual experts

who are willing and able to give advice on the deep
things of the soul as that there should be specialists
to whom we apply for advice in regard to obscure and
virulent maladies of the body. As it is, the work of
confession, and of responsive help in sympathy and
advice, is probably overtaken to some extent in the
confidences of Christian friendship in which a minister
shares, but there is doubtless room for a better
organisation of the efforts which St. James had in
view within the life of the Church when he counselled
confessing faults one to another.

The third part of a genuine repentance is to bring
forth fruits meet for repentance. In relation to actual
sins of a heinous kind this takes the form of reparation. A cardinal maxim of the subject is laid down
by the King in *Hamlet*—that one does not truly
repent if he continues to reap the advantages which
he derived from the sinful act. If the sin has been
of the nature of a wrong, the duty is to make reparation to the person who was wronged. The Roman
Catholic Church developed from this root the part of
its sacrament of Penance, according to which it ap-
pertains to the priest to prescribe to the penitent a
satisfaction which may take the form of masses, of
self-mortification, of almsgiving, and of other forms
of Christian liberality. The Protestant conscience repudiated the doctrine of satisfaction and on the good
ground that it was so expounded, or at least popularly
so understood, as to imply that something needs to
be added to the atoning sacrifice of Christ in order

to secure a full and free forgiveness of former sins. But while the name of a satisfaction may very properly be dropped, and all idea of acquiring merit before God must be rigidly excluded, it may be thought that the idea is a sound one that an act or a course of heinous sin ought to be followed by an appropriate reparation. If a man was formerly a drunkard, the appropriate reparation is to throw himself ardently into the cause of temperance. If he was once a blasphemer like St. Paul, he may well, like the apostle, desire to become a preacher of the gospel. If he once made a fortune by questionable methods, he may well think no disposition of his ill-gotten wealth so appropriate as to give or bequeath it to some class of the poor who are the victims of social injustice. Lesser sins will suggest lesser, but it may be not less suitable, forms of reparation.

In the case of a sinful habit the fruit of a true repentance obviously is that we break off the habit. The end of repentance is reformation or amendment of life. But the advice is not easy to act on. Many find it extremely difficult to abandon even a secondary habit, and it becomes much more difficult when it is a question of habits—such as selfishness, or pride, or temper, or sloth, which have become part of the staple of our character. The subject is too large to be adequately treated now, but we may at least give the two great maxims which bear upon the matter. One is that, in order to a serious effort at self-amendment, we need a fresh impulse and uplift from the

Spirit of God, which is to be sought in humble prayer. The other is that if we are trying to overcome an evil habit we must endeavour by practice and repetition to form a good habit to take the place of the bad one.

Why should we repent of the repeated transgression and of the evil habit? The answer is easy in the case of the more heinous sort: according to the Scriptures there are sins of such enormity that persistence in them is convincing proof that we are not in the state of grace which gives us the assurance of acceptance with God, and the hope of everlasting life. In the case of the less heinous faults the Protestant is apt to argue that if he is in a state of grace he will be saved in spite of them, and that if he is not saved they will not make his condition any worse. The Roman Catholic doctrine seems more salutary, as it holds out the threat that, though the sins may be venial, they may be expected to prolong the imprisonment in Purgatory and add to its pains. But even if one reject the Roman Catholic ideas of Purgatory, it does not follow that it will make no difference in the eternal world whether we were really sanctified or of the number of those who were scarcely saved. And in any case we are urged by the whole scope of the gospel, by love to Christ, by gratitude, by the sense of Christian honour, to place ourselves in fullest accord with the will of Him who died that " He might redeem us from all iniquity, and purify us unto Himself a peculiar people zealous of good works." Amen.

VIII.

THE RECORDING BOOKS.

"For there is nothing covered, that shall not be revealed; neither hid, that shall not be known."—LUKE xii. 2.

"And the books were opened."—REVELATION xx. 12.

SOME people are at their best when they think they are unobserved, and many more are at their worst. Some undoubtedly there are who have virtues and graces that shun the light of day. There are those whose affection for wife and child shrinks from any public display; those who might be thought irreligious until in some place apart they were discovered on their knees; and even those to whom the fact that an action can be done by stealth is an additional argument for giving a large subscription or helping a brother in distress. Obviously, however, the darkness is responsible for more evil than good. When we come to be tried, one of the strongest of the persuasives of the Tempter is that "no one need ever know"; and only too often does it happen, when a man enters into a world of new surroundings and unknown faces, that the hitherto irreproachable life is seen to have been inspired, not by the fear of doing wrong, but only by the fear of being discovered. There is a classical fable of a man who came into possession of a magical ring, which had the property of rendering him invisible, and who, because of the immunity from detection and punishment which he thus secured, forthwith deteriorated into a rogue and a villain. There is the Biblical story of Achan, a man doubtless as honest as his comrades, until he lit upon a wedge of gold and a Babylonish garment, with no witnesses at hand save the men slain in the fall of Jericho, and, overpowered by the temptation of secrecy, he carried off the unlawful spoil and buried it in a hole in the tent. And though it would be a libel on human nature to say that these examples hold good of man as man in everyday life, the temptation of secrecy certainly destroys its thousands and hundreds of thousands. The shop - boy or servant girl who ended as a thief pocketed the first article or coin because it would never be missed; the broken-down sensualist, who once came to the great city clothed with innocence, drifted into disreputable company because the village home and the lynx-eyed neighbours were a hundred miles away; another developed into a drunkard because the thing was done in a corner; in short, no small proportion of the vice that is in the world, and still more of its dishonesty, is due to the fact that it is supposed that it will never be found out.

This supposition, now, which is at the root of so much wrong-doing, is declared in Scripture to be an utter delusion. The permanent concealment of anything, it repeatedly affirms, is impossible. There is a divine government of the world, and one of its laws is that there is nothing hid that shall not be known. There takes place, in the case of each individual, a process of self-disclosure, which is begun here and consummated hereafter. Even in this world the discovery is fuller than is commonly supposed, so that most evil-doers would be startled if they only knew how little successful they have been in hiding anything important about themselves, or in seriously deceiving the judgment of those with whom they are closely associated. But the solemnity of the Scriptural teaching is further enhanced by its pointing to a future state of existence in which the last pretence of a mask will be torn from the face, and the whole life will be laid open to scrutiny and judgment. Of this last and completing stage Christ was partly thinking when He said that "there is nothing covered which shall not be revealed"; and on it the thoughts of the seer of Patmos were wholly fixed when, waking out of his apocalyptic vision, he wrote that "the books were opened."

The doctrine of the unconcealable, as it may be termed, is one of the most important and practical of the fundamental truths of religion, and, if I mistake not, the mere assertion of it finds a corroborative echo in the general conscience of mankind. It may, however, serve to impress it more forcibly upon the mind if we reflect upon the means which exist for preserving evidence of our character and conduct during the days of our life on earth. That such means or machinery exists is not open to doubt. Adopting the metaphor of the Book of Revelation, we may say that there are at least three books in which the story of our lives is being written from day to day, and from which our deeds, our words, and even our thoughts may be ascertainable in a future period of existence. The first book is the Memory of God, the second is the Memory of the World, the third is the Memory of the Self; and of these we shall speak in order.

I.

THE LIST OF THE RECORDING BOOKS.

1. The witness which preserves the most full and faithful record of our lives is the Memory of God. There is a popular idea of a recording angel whose business is to write in a mighty book the story of our life, and who as he writes now rejoices as only the angels rejoice, and now blurs the page with his tears. And though this conception is of course a creation of the imagination, the picture at least expresses the religious verity, to some so dreadful, to others so comfortable, that the God with whom we have to do is the God of the all-seeing eye and of the unerring memory. It serves to remind us of the fact that God, the everywhere present, is acquainted with all our ways, reads our motives, weighs our words, judges our actions; and that all that He knows of us is committed to a memory which holds what is entrusted to it with the grasp of Omnipotence. It was characteristic of the older piety of the English-speaking world that men had an intensely realising sense of the all-seeing and never-slumbering God; and it would be difficult to exaggerate the effect of this realisation in the production of a strong type of moral character, and in the investiture of life with a habitual earnestness and solemnity. In particular what was felt above all to give to death the character of the King of Terrors was that it brought a man into the nearer presence of Him who had followed him through every stage of his journey between the cradle and the grave—a Being from whom no secrets had been hid, whom no precautions deceived, and with whom no subterfuges had availed.

2. The second of the recording books is the Memory of the World. This book, when examined, is found to consist of two volumes. What we may describe as the first volume is the memory of our fellow-creatures so far as it carries a recollection of our actions and a judgment upon our character. It is curious to reflect how various and even conflicting are the impressions which we must have made upon the different persons, and groups of persons, with whom we have been associated in the ever-changing scenes and circumstances of our earthly life. Some of these, no doubt,

preserve a recollection of us which is a specimen of good-natured flattery—members of our family circle, it may be, whose affection transfigured us; or intimate friends who had the gift of drawing out what was best in us, and lifting us to our highest levels; or passing acquaintances who knew us only in connection with some act or speech of unwonted courage or generosity, and who went their way cherishing that incident as the index to our whole life. Others, again, whose opportunities were limited to seeing only one of the worst aspects of our character, have gone on their way to think of us, when they think of us at all, with a dislike or a contempt that is as unmerited as the admiration of the first. But when an average is struck between these two extremes there remains a judgment, framed by the majority of those who have known us, which is based on a wonderfully just impression of our life; so that it is not without good ground that men value, next to the approving judgment of God, and of their own consciences, a favourable verdict from the living memory of mankind.

The second volume may be called the unconscious memory of the world. By this I mean the record of our actions which will be preserved by the inanimate universe. Part of such record may be the inscription on a tombstone which will tell that in such a year we were born, and in such a year we died, and which, in the course of a few generations, will be obliterated. But there is reason to believe than even commonplace people leave behind them fuller inscriptions than the brief epitaph, and leave them on monuments more enduring than the memorial tablet of stone. In a remarkable book entitled *The Unseen Universe*, which aroused much attention among the students of twenty years ago, two well-known scientists propounded the speculation that we are in contact with an unseen universe which registers and preserves impressions of the actors who cross the stage of human history. The inventions of the nineteenth century help to make the idea clearer. We no longer feel it to be marvellous that the photographic plate should faithfully produce the expression of a particular mood, or that our words should be given back to us, with the peculiarities of tone and accent, by the help of a phonograph ; and it makes no excessive demand on our credulity to suppose that we leave traces of ourselves on other surfaces which it may be possible for the denizens of the unseen universe to handle and decipher. In the book to which I have referred it is suggested that in this way it may be possible in another life to recover words and sayings of Christ during His earthly ministry which have been omitted from the brief record of the written Gospels; and those who shall make a search in the mystic records may be expected to find a transcript of words and deeds of others that redound, some to the glory of the grace of God, some to the shame and the humiliation of sinful men.

3. The third of the recording books is the Memory

of the Self.   This also exists in two volumes—the conscious and the unconscious memory.

By the conscious I mean the memory proper —that strange power of the mind in virtue of which it can make the things of the past seem to belong once more to the present, or to differ from them in vividness only by so much as the moonlit differs from the sunlit world.   It does not appear on examination that memory is the feeble and inaccurate instrument which is popularly supposed.   Many things seem to be lost in it, as many are lost in the deep wide sea, but it may well be true that it, like the sea, is destined to give up all the dead that are in it.   It is said that it often happens that, in the moment when one is on the brink of sudden death, there takes place a swift rush before the mind's eye of the events of the past life; and even in less high-strung moods an incident or a picture will return without any effort to recover it, and with startling minuteness and clearness, out of long oblivion.   " I am convinced," wrote De Quincey, " that the dread book of account is in fact the mind itself of the individual, and that there is no such thing as forgetting possible."   As the stars temporarily disappear when the sun shines, so many things are forgotten when fresh interests engage the attention; but everything that was once in the mind can return as surely as the stars again shine out in the firmament when the sun has gone down.   What is certain is that even on earth memory has power to give us a foretaste of heaven or hell, and this being so it may well be believed that it has of itself power to build for us a heaven, or to furnish for us a hell, in the eternal world.

There is also the unconscious memory which we bear about with us in the shape of our character. What we are at any given time, especially in middle life and in old age, is a monument of the kind of life we have lived, and of the quality of the actions which we have performed. Every deliberate act, certainly every habit, may be said to imprint markings upon the soul. I am not here thinking so much of the way in which a man's conduct leaves its impress upon the form and the countenances—though this is part of it, so that with advancing years the appearance often becomes a mirror of the tenor of one's past. I am thinking rather of the spiritual substance of the soul, upon which our conduct stamps a more vigorous and faithful impress than it leaves upon the material of flesh and blood. Founding upon this idea Plato taught that, when our spirits escape from the prison-house of the body, they will appear in the unseen world in such form as will reveal to its inhabitants the nature of the life which we led on earth. In a famous passage of the *Republic* he pictures a tyrant coming before the judges of the dead. They put no questions—as to his country, his name, his station; they call no witnesses; they hear no pleader; the evidence is before them in the mere appearance of the shade, in a visible deformity which speaks to a life of lies, in sores and bruises which testify of sensuality and cruelty; and without debate the judges agree upon the verdict, and consign him to his place and portion of appropriate punishment. Stripped of its imaginative elements this picture embodies one of the most certain truths of human nature. In all our actions, and not least in our thoughts and plans, we are labouring at the making of ourselves, and when our character is matured it is a storied monument of our past. Just as the history of the remote past of our earth is re-told by the scientist from his inspection of the appearance on the rocks, so may it be possible for the science of the unseen world, when bringing its scrutiny to bear upon the souls that arrive from our world, to read the tracings that tell of the sins that at one time injured and stained us, but also to find evidence of virtues and graces that blushed unseen, and of Christlike deeds that flourished in the shade.

II.

THE CONSOLATIONS AND LIMITATIONS OF THE GOSPEL.

We now proceed to consider whether, and in what way, the records which have been discussed are reckoned with in the gospel of Jesus Christ. As a fact, the gospel recognises at least two of them as threatening consequences which constitute a large part of the religious distress of man, and from which Christ came to give us release.

1. We have spoken of the memory of God, and of the apprehensions with which the thought of it should fill the mind of the sinner; and over against it there is set in the gospel, as the corresponding blessing, the boon of the forgiveness of sins. By this is not meant that God can entirely forget our sins; this is doubtless impossible: what is meant, and it is of equal value, is that God is willing to act towards us as if He did not remember them, to deal with repentant sinners as if no sinful past had ever divided them, to receive them to the footing of sons, and to bestow upon them all blessings which are prompted by the love of a Heavenly Father. As directly and boldly, moreover, the gospel grapples with the second fact to which reference was made in describing the tendency of a sinful life to write its record in a depraved and enslaved character. The message of the gospel is that no character can be regarded as utterly fixed in evil, no chain of bad habits as unbreakable; that there is a divine power, a new supernatural life, which God is willing to communicate by the Holy Spirit to them that ask Him, and which not only purifies the affections, but admits to the glorious liberty of the children of God. And in these two truths we have those aspects of the gospel which are peculiarly designed for the consolation of the old. They may feel that they have wandered far and sinned deeply, they may think that they have as little strength left as they have opportunity to do otherwise than they have done; but God, of His great mercy

and grace, chides their fears, and admonishes them
that if only they can sorrow, and trust like a little
child in His mercy, they will be saved from the worst
consequences of their sins by the Father, who is not only
faithful and just to forgive us our sins for Christ's sake,
but who also by the Spirit makes all things new.

2. On the other hand, the course of reflection
which we have pursued may well suggest a warning,
and that specially for those who are younger, as to
the limitations of the gospel. It reminds us that
those who sin deeply against themselves and against
society may readily find that they have brought
upon themselves penalties from which there is no
escape. From the memory of the world, as it has
been termed, the record of evil-doing will not readily
disappear. We may confine our view at this stage
to the remembrance of us which is preserved by our
fellow-man; and when we think of this, it is clear
that it is only too easy to act so foolishly or wickedly
that society will hardly forget or forgive. The
esteem of our fellow-men is a valuable possession;
but it is as fragile as some vase of brittle ware; let
it once be broken, then, piece it together as labori-
ously as we may, it can never again be as beautiful
as it was. The stigma of a crime can hardly be lived
down; but, short of this, if a man be guilty of one
flagrant and notorious act of foolishness, intemper-
ance, or untruthfulness, though he may be vastly
better than that suggests, the world, which does not
draw fine distinctions, will not think so. In the

light of that he is remembered, by it he is judged, even as Esau, though he doubtless had many excellent qualities, passed into history as the typical fool—the man who sold his birthright for a supper. It may even be observed that a bad reputation tends to get worse of its own accord, just as Esau, who to begin with was nothing worse than a fool, has come to be described, by the time the story reaches the age of the Apostles, as a profane person and a fornicator. To the young, therefore, I would say, guard strictly and jealously the possession of a good name, lest you realise in sorrowful experience that, if there is nothing more easily lost, there is nothing harder to recover, and that in respect of it, as in Esau's case, there may be found no place of repentance though you seek it carefully with tears.

Another limitation of the gospel may be found in the implacableness of a man's own memory. The belief in the forgiveness of sins by God will not wholly rob memory of the sting wherewith it torments those who have once made of it an enemy. This seems clear enough if we reflect upon such a story as that told in the Parable of the Prodigal Son, in which God is represented as rejoicing to bestow upon the penitent a forgiveness as full as love may grant. The Jewish father, who stands for God, ran and fell upon the neck of the returning prodigal, but do we think it would be easy for him to forgive himself? Must he not for many a year have felt remorse as he recalled the years which the canker-worm had eaten,

8

as he thought of the patrimony which had been squandered and which was not replaced, as he traced out the after-career of the companions whom he had once convoyed on the way to ruin, or mourned, it might be, for a mother whose grey hairs he had brought down with sorrow to the grave. I will tell young men what they shall fear: they are to fear memory with its power to torture those who once forgot God and the future.

The Doctrine of the Unconcealable has commonly been used as the terror of the Lord to dissuade men from practising the works of darkness. But it would be to wrong God, and to be unjust to human nature, to assume that it possesses only a terrifying aspect. There are those to whom the thought, "Thou God seest me," is less a source of fear than a spring of consolation. There are those to whom it appears to be, not so much a threat as a promise, that "there is nothing covered that shall not be revealed, neither hid that shall not be known." It is their comfort to know that they are beset behind and before by one in whom there dwells a sympathy as boundless as His knowledge is exact. They are glad to think that, while men may misunderstand and misrepresent, they have to do ultimately with one who makes no mistakes either as to fact or motive. They can plead in self-vindication, "Lord, Thou knowest all things, Thou knowest that I love Thee." The Day of Judgment may suggest, not the humiliations of exposure and the horrors of doom, but the divine consideration and magnanimity of Christ the Judge, who will fasten even upon the little deeds of kindness —the cup of cold water, the crust of bread, the visit to the house of mourning—and making mention of these things that they had forgotten will say, " Forasmuch as ye did it unto one of the least of these my brethren, ye did it unto me."   Amen.

IX.

THE DESCENT INTO HELL.

"He went and preached unto the spirits in prison; which some-time were disobedient."—1 PETER iii. 19, 20.

IN listening to the public recitation of the Apostles' Creed one sometimes has the impression that the voice of the congregation falters when it repeats—" He descended into Hell." It is as if some shivered at the suggestion of some unspeakable mystery, or that they paused in the joyful and confident confession to ask themselves, "Do I really believe this?" or at least, "Do I know what I am confessing?"

There is some excuse if we are puzzled to know what it exactly means. The article was first inserted in a second edition of the Apostles' Creed as enlarged about 500 years after Christ, and since it was inserted it has been interpreted in many different ways. What it certainly does not mean is what many who use the words suppose to be its obvious meaning. By Hell is popularly understood the place of everlasting torment; and it is natural to suppose that what is taught is that Christ after His death went down to the abode of devils and of lost souls; and further, that as Christ endured the penalty of our sins He there endured for a season in our stead the sufferings of the damned. But this was not the idea of those who first framed the article, nor has it been held in this precise form by any representative teachers of the Christian Church.

There are three questions which are raised in regard to the descent of Christ into Hell. The first is, When did this event take place? The second is, Where did it take place? The third is, Why did it take place? What end did it serve? We shall consider first the principal views which have been held in the Church; next, the light thrown on the subject by Scripture; and lastly, some of the inferences which are supported by the chief scriptural references as we understand them.

I.

ECCLESIASTICAL INTERPRETATIONS.

1. The view of many of the Christian Fathers was that Christ went to the under-world in order to release the patriarchs of the old dispensation from a lower sphere, and conduct them to the Heaven of bliss. They held that there was a place lying between Heaven and Hell, a "limbo of the fathers," in which the Old Testament saints were kept in ward until the advent of the Messiah. What Christ

did was to descend to this prison-house, to "break
in pieces the gates of brass, and cut in sunder the
bars of iron," and to "bring forth the prisoners
out of the pit, wherein there was no water."
Irenæus says he heard from those who had been
disciples of the Apostles "that the Lord descended
to the places beneath the earth preaching His
advent, and declaring remission of sins to just men,
prophets, and patriarchs, who had foretold His
advent and obeyed it." This opinion has been
widely held in the Anglican Church. Jeremy Taylor
pictures the scene of joy "in the dark and un-
discerned mansions, when the prisoners of hope,
lying in the lake in which there was no water, saw
their Redeemer come to change their condition into
the neighbourhood of glory." The conception was
rejected by the old Protestant theologians because
they found no evidence in Scripture that there is
any abode of departed spirits except a Heaven of
perfected holiness and happiness, and a Hell of
wickedness and torment. They had, therefore, to
find a meaning for the clause which would be consistent with the assumption that Hell must here be
understood as the place of everlasting punishment.

2. The theory of Martin Luther was that Christ
descended to Hell properly so called, but in the
guise of a conqueror, not of a victim. The purpose
of the descent was, he supposed, to manifest His
triumph over Satan, and to overthrow his power
in the very citadel of his empire. "We believe,"

as it runs in a Lutheran Confession, "that Christ, after being buried, descended into Hell, vanquished Satan, overthrew the Kingdom of Darkness, and deprived Satan of all power and dominion." As to the nature of the conflict, and the way in which Satan was vanquished, they professed no knowledge. It was no doubt a sublime conception that the Christ, who was thought by men and devils to have been crushed on Calvary, forthwith appeared in the realm of darkness with a new challenge, and in irresistible might; and it derived some support from the scriptural passages in which Christ's work is described as a victory over Satan. On the other hand, it is not a very spiritual idea that Christ held a triumphal procession, somewhat after the pattern of Roman generals, to emphasise the glory of the conqueror and the humiliation of the vanquished. Moreover, in the most relevant passage, Christ is said to have preached the gospel, an expression which does not fit in with the idea of a punitive invasion and a pageant of triumph.

3. Calvin interpreted the descent into Hell as an experience of Christ when our sins were laid upon Him. He understood by it the descent of Christ in spirit into the utmost depths of distress and anguish. The time, however, was before He gave up the ghost upon the cross. The purpose of it was that Christ should undergo the last extremity of suffering for the sins of the world, and this was supposed to take place when in a manner He descended into Hell in the

agony of Gethsemane, and in the desertion on the Cross of Calvary. To this view it was naturally objected that it was inconsistent with the order of events in the Creed, which should in that case have run, "descended into Hell, crucified, dead, and buried." Calvin replied, though not very convincingly, that the order of the Creed is not necessarily chronological, that it first enumerates the events which occurred in the sight of men, and thereafter speaks of the invisible and incomprehensible experience which took place in the sight and under the judgment of God. He also says that it is natural that the descent into Hell, as being the most important, is properly put last to mark the climax of the events of the Passion. In general it may be said that Calvin's view is a restatement of a great truth, namely, that Christ offered a sacrifice in the experiences of His passion, which was accepted by God as the sacrifice for the world's sin. But it is certain that this is not what was meant by the framers of the Creed, and the article would also be a very awkward and misleading form of words for expressing what is true in Calvin's idea. Carlyle was fond of saying of a man who had passed through great tribulation of soul that he had been in Hell, but such a figure of speech was not suitable for the Creed, and cannot be honestly extracted from it.

4. Even the great authority of Calvin was not able to impose his interpretation upon the Reformed Churches. The doctrine of the Church of

Scotland is that "Christ's humiliation after His death consisted in His being buried, and continuing in the state of the dead, and in the power of death, till the third day." To say that Christ descended into Hell would thus be a mere repetition of the statement that He died and was buried, and would be equivalent to saying that during this time He was really dead, and that His spirit was in the place prepared for Him by God. In other words, it means that Christ went to the place to which those go after death who die in a state of grace. When, therefore, we repeat the Creed,, the clause "He descended into Hell" means no more, it was taught, and was not intended to mean more, than that Christ really died on the cross, leaving it to us to supply anything further from our general knowledge of the condition of the blessed dead. But we should certainly think it a strange mode of expression to say of one of our departed friends, who had, we trusted, gone to Heaven, that he had descended into Hell; and if this is all the meaning which it had when asserted of Christ, it must be said that the clause is unhappily phrased, and even culpably misleading to the popular understanding.

II.

THE NEW TESTAMENT REFERENCES.

The texts directly bearing on the subject are not numerous. One is the promise of our Lord to the penitent robber: "To-day shalt thou be with me in Paradise" (Luke xxiii. 43). The word Paradise must have spoken comfort and hope to the dying thief, but it may have meant less than the highest Heaven. There is a quotation from the Psalms, quoted by the early Christians: "Thou wilt not leave my soul in hell, neither wilt thou suffer thine Holy One to see corruption" (Acts ii. 27). In the Revised Version it is called Hades, which in the Old Testament was used to describe the whole realm of the dead, without distinction of Heaven and Hell. St. Paul has a vague reference: "Now that he ascended, what is it but that he also descended first into the lower parts of the earth?" (Eph. iv. 9). The subject seems to be most definitely in view in two passages of the First Epistle of Peter. "Christ being put to death in the flesh, but quickened in the spirit, by which also he went and preached unto the spirits in prison, which aforetime were disobedient, when the long-suffering of God waited in the days of Noah" (1 Pet. iii. 18–20). It is also said, obviously with the same reference, that "the gospel was preached even to the dead" (1 Pet. iv. 6).

In dealing with the two last passages it has usually been assumed by Protestant divines that the settled teaching of Scripture is that there are only two abodes of departed spirits—a Heaven in which there is nothing more to fear, and a Hell in which there is nothing more to hope, and that there can be here no suggestion of a third abode. They therefore looked for an explanation which would connect the preaching of Christ to "the spirits in prison" with some time other than the day following Christ's death, and some place other than Hell. The meaning of the dark passage has usually been said to be that the time when Christ preached to the spirits in prison was the age of the Flood, that the persons whom He addressed were the disobedient of that time, and that the method of His preaching was to appeal to them through the Spirit which inspired and spoke by Noah as a preacher of repentance. But in the Epistle the writer gives a sequence of events in the life of Christ—suffered, died, went and preached, rose again, went to Heaven—and it is very unnatural to suppose that he includes in the list one event which, instead of falling within this cycle of events, took place in the antediluvian world. Similarly with the passage in which it is said that the gospel was preached to the dead. As the idea of preaching the gospel to souls after death conflicted with the belief that the decisions taken during our earthly life are final, it was explained that it meant no more than if a minister should say that he had preached to thousands of the dead—meaning people who were by this time in their graves. But the apostle must seem to a candid reader to have in view those who were dead at the time when the preaching was addressed to them. The most probable and indeed natural interpretation is that our Lord did, after His death on Calvary, descend to the abode of departed spirits, and preach the gospel at least to some of an

earlier generation who, when they were alive, had
disobeyed the word of God.

III.

DOCTRINAL AND PRACTICAL CONSEQUENCES.

The descent into Hell is not a mere matter of
idle speculation and barren controversy. It has
an intimate bearing upon a question of the deepest
religious interest—a question which is always with us,
and which, in the circumstances of the present time,
burdens and even torments many minds and hearts.

It has a very close bearing upon the problem of
future destinies. We have all reflected more or less
upon the question as to what is to be our portion in
the next world. We have been forced to reflect
upon it when relatives and friends have passed from
our society into the realm of the unseen. With
special emphasis and solemnity has the question
revived in these times, when men have been called
to face the deadly hazards of war, and tens of
thousands have been cut off in the promise of their
youth, or in the midst of their years, by a violent
and untimely death. Many have been distressed or
repelled by the doctrine of their Church on the
subject, and are asking if that doctrine is really true.
The traditional conception is that those who die
are separated at death into two companies — the
saved and the unsaved, that the destiny of both

classes is settled irrevocably at death, and that after death the souls of the saved do immediately pass to the glory, the bliss, and the perfected holiness of Heaven, while the unsaved are forthwith consigned to the place of everlasting punishment. The tests by which they are separated into the two companies are repentance unto life and faith in Jesus Christ. The saved are those who, under a deep sense of their sin, and apprehension of the mercy of God in Christ (whereby they receive and rest upon Christ alone for salvation), have turned from their sins unto God with full purpose of, and endeavour after, new obedience. It will, now, hardly be disputed that a very large number of people, even of good Christian people, have broken in one way if not in another with this scheme of thought. After attending the funeral service of an ordinary member of society we may well find ourselves asking if the reflections and the consolations of most Protestant ministers are generally governed by the premises and the tests which have just been explained. The dissent from the old positions may take either of two lines.

Usually it is assumed that the traditional view is true, in so far as it teaches that there is a Heaven and a Hell, and that destiny is settled at death ; and the breach with the old ideas takes the form of altering the tests, of so widening and liberalising them, that practically every one who has not been a notorious evil-liver is assumed to have been received to the mercy of God, and to have obtained an immediate and abundant entrance into the Kingdom of Heaven. We have felt strongly impelled to lower the standard so as to meet the case of all who have enjoyed the respect of society, and won the affection of friends and kin; and in the special conditions of the present time many have heartily adopted what is said to be the soldier's creed—that those who die in battle for their country are forthwith translated into Heaven. But this solution, easy and tempting as it is, is beset by serious difficulties. Many of those who die, however worthy they may have been of our affection and our admiration, were not fit for Heaven—would not themselves feel at home in its atmosphere of worship and holiness; and though we may assume such a transformation in them as would make them meet to take their place among angels and saints, this seems to involve such a breach of continuity as to imperil their personal identity, and also to set forth Death rather than Christ as the Saviour of mankind. Above all, it is a very serious modification of the gospel to reduce the conditions of salvation from the lofty Biblical demands of repentance unto life and faith in Jesus Christ to the lax terms which will fit even a very commonplace average of character, experience, and conduct.

The alternative method of relief is to retain the tests in something of their original elevation and rigour, but to question the assumptions that the only abodes of the departed are Heaven and Hell, and that with the departure from earth there is a final determination of the eternal destiny. The conception is that there is in addition an abode such as the Hades of the Old Testament, in which there take place further processes of discipline for those not yet fit for Heaven, and in which also there are given further opportunities of decision to those who could not reasonably be claimed by the devil and his angels for a true and eternal Hell. On this view there are still those of whom we can reasonably hope that they immediately pass into glory. Those who can credibly be described as saved, but who are scarcely saved, would have a further discipline designed to make them meet, by the strengthening of faith and the ennoblement of character, for entering upon the full inheritance of the blessed. For those who could not be described as saved in any real sense of the word, while yet they might fall far short of diabolical defiance and wickedness, there would be a further probation, in which it would be ensured that previous lack of opportunity or understanding would be redressed, and the terms of the gospel would be clearly and cogently addressed to their minds and consciences. Such ideas derive not a little support from the instincts of the human heart, from the principle of the continuity of human experience, and from consideration of the implications of the Fatherhood of God. The striking passage from the First Epistle of Peter is evidence that even in the apostolic age the Christian mind was drawn in this direction. The writer believed that the gospel was preached after death to men of the old dispensation—

and not merely to patriarchs, but to those who in a corrupt age had died in unbelief and disobedience. Further, as there is no intelligible reason why special mercy should have been shown to the sinners of the days of Noah, it may fairly be supposed that these stand as representatives of the pre-Christian world in general. And yet again, if the heathen dying without the knowledge of Christ and His gospel are accorded a further probation, the same hope may be cherished at least in regard to those numberless persons who lived in a nominally Christian world, but whom the gospel never reached in any real and effective sense. And if the gates of mercy are opened thus wide, it is an easy step to the position that there is a future probation which includes in its scope practically all men—at least all who when they left this earth were not yet devils but human beings.

Against the doctrine of future probation, which is favoured by the article of Christ's descent into Hell, grave objections have been urged. Scripture, it is held, says nothing in the clear passages in support of the view. But as it is the way of prophecy—and the doctrine of the future state is of the nature of prophecy—that it does not give us measures of distance in time or place, it may well be that Scripture only witnesses to final consummations and ignores the opportunities and experiences of the regions which lie between death and the final issues. It is also objected that the Bible positively contradicts the hope of a future probation by repeated declarations in varying form that "now is the accepted time, now is the day of salvation." It is added that it is only when we accept this teaching that we are likely to value and use our life as we ought. If we really believe that the day of our earthly life is the day of visitation that will determine and colour our unending future, we shall be moved to a great seriousness in the use of it; if we do not so believe, we shall be tempted to make light of it, and to squander our powers and opportunities. But the spiritual danger of the theory of probation has been exaggerated. Many of the solemn decisions which we take in regard to our life on earth entail consequences which are not irreparable, but we may still feel that it matters a very great deal what is the nature of the decisions that we take. Many men have been very successful in making up leeway at a later date though they neglected their opportunities at school, but a father refuses to admit that his boy properly argues that it does not in the least matter whether he neglects his education or not. Some men, after having been drunkards or profligates in youth, have reformed in later life, but few therefore think of saying that it makes no difference whether a man does or does not waste in dissipation the golden years of youth. And in like fashion, even if we think that the theory of future probation is probable, we ought still to be assured that the use which we make of our earthly life will determine the character with which we start, and the conditions under

9

which we resume in the next stage of our existence, and also affect our prospects for eternity.

The teaching of the Scriptures in regard to the future state is marked by two features—a great certainty as to the fact of a life to come and as to the conditions of eternal salvation, and an equally striking reticence in regard to secondary conditions and problems. The certainties are—on the positive side, that the gift of God is eternal life through Jesus Christ our Lord ; on the negative side, that those who are in alienation from God, and under the pollution and the dominion of sin, are even now under the wrath of God, and must look forward, unless and until they repent, to the manifestation of a greater wrath to come. These are the things which it vitally concerns us to know, and they have been made abundantly clear and assured. But the hand of God has only lifted a corner of the veil. As to the ultimate fate of those who die unsaved, it is the opinion of many devout students, with whom I agree, that we have not materials for dogmatising. We do not know whether, if there should be a further day of grace, some would resist God to the end; and we do not know whether the finally impenitent, if such there be, will be annihilated or live on in a Hell. In particular, we must say in regard to the intermediate state that we have no sure knowledge—only guesses and hopes. Even if St. Peter meant what we have taken him to mean, we cannot suppose that the difficult passage was given as a special revelation to light up the dark region : at the most it lends support to an inference from the verities of the Christian faith, and in particular from the patient love of God and the known fidelity of Christ, that there will be a further probation for those who died in unbelief. God meant us to live our lives with a large element of dubiety and ignorance alongside of the great certitudes. One reason doubtless was that there is an uncertainty which has unique value as a spiritual discipline, not only for those who feel that there is nothing they fear more than the terror of the darkness, but also for those who because of their ignorance cling closer to their God and Saviour. Also it may be that it is one of the joys of the fatherly heart of God to keep in store a world of merciful surprises, as He certainly has also in store many painful surprises, for the children of His human family. Amen.

X

THE PRESBYTERIAN HERITAGE.

"Unto the angel of the church of Ephesus write."—REVELA-TION ii. 1.

"Neglect not the gift that is in thee, which was given thee by prophecy, with the laying on of the hands of the presbytery."—1 TIMOTHY iv. 14.

I PROPOSE in this sermon to set forth some of the salient features of that type of Christianity which is known as Presbyterianism, and which has its headquarters in Scotland and its chief example in the Church of our fathers. We may suitably take as our starting-point the message of St. John to the Church in Ephesus, because in many points his epistle holds up a mirror to ourselves, and reminds us both of the excellences and of the shortcomings of the Scottish Church. St. John praised the Church in Ephesus because it "tried them which said they were apostles and were not, and found them liars"; and this has its counterpart in the zeal for sound doctrine which has been prominent in the testimony of most of its great preachers. He also reckons it among their virtues that they hated the deeds of the Nicolaitanes, and this corresponds to the intense moral earnestness of our best periods, and the stern discipline by which the Church sought to guard the purity of its membership.   He further praises the Church in Ephesus for that it had " borne and had patience and had not fainted "—which history has been repeated in the persecutions of our Church, and in the heroism and self-sacrifice which they evoked, the only difference being that we should hardly single out patience as a distinctive quality of our Reforming and Covenanting heroes in their times of trial.   Again, like its prototype in Ephesus the Scottish Church has abounded in works and in labour, so that its fame has gone abroad throughout the world because of the part taken by so large a proportion of its members in the work of the congregation, and especially because of the magnificence of the collective contribution which is made by our little country in support of the enterprise of Foreign Missions.   On the other hand, the commendation of the Scottish Church, like that of its ancient prototype, falls to be qualified by a " nevertheless." With its zeal for doctrine and principle, it sometimes showed a want of spiritual insight in failing to discriminate between what was of primary and what of secondary importance; and with all its strength, heroism, and moral earnestness it seems to have imperfectly grasped the bearings of Christian liberty, and to have insufficiently appreciated the spirit of the Sermon on the Mount.   Especially may it be thought that in recent times there has been some decline in the fervour of religious feeling which formerly glowed so brightly and ardently in passionate devotion to Christ and in zeal for the salvation of souls, and that the rebuke of the apostle has point against us as well as them of Ephesus: "I have somewhat against thee, because thou hast left thy first love"!

It is not very common for a Scottish minister to discourse upon Presbyterianism. The concrete reality of the Church of Scotland, or of the United Free Church, is deeply seated in the affections, and commands the fervent loyalty, of many who are unmoved by the abstract name which is the symbol of their theological and ecclesiastical principles. In Scotland, moreover, we commonly suppose that Presbyterianism has been and is so large and beneficent a fact in our national life, that its nature, its merits, and its achievements can be taken for granted. More recently, however, an impetus has come from two different sides which has given to the subject a fresh interest. One is a controversy which has recently raged in England as to whether it was or was not a scandal that, at a missionary conference in South Africa, an Anglican bishop sat down at the Communion Table along with ministers and members of the Church of Scotland. The other and more effective stimulus has proceeded from the Conferences between the two great Presbyterian Churches, which have led them to reflect on their common inheritance.

What does Presbyterianism stand for? What special claim has it on our affections and our service?

I.

THE TYPE OF ECCLESIASTICAL CONSTITUTION.

The feature which has given to Presbyterianism its name is not one which is of the first importance in a religious point of view. It is, that it recognises only one order of ministers—presbyters or bishops —and that these ministers, who are of equal status, exercise supreme authority under Christ in the management of spiritual and ecclesiastical affairs. There is an aristocratic type of constitution represented by the Church of England, which has three orders of clergy, and vests the supreme power in the College of Bishops ; the monarchical type is represented by the Roman Catholic Church, which asserts the sovereign authority and infallibility of the Bishop of Rome ; while Presbyterianism, with its principle of ministerial equality, and its government by Kirk-Session, Presbytery, Synod, and Assembly, represents the democratic type of ecclesiastical polity. It is right, indeed, to say that few Presbyterians now take the high ground of affirming that it was given as matter of divine revelation that Presbytery is the one lawful form of Church government. We recognise that Christ left a great deal of detail in the way of ecclesiastical organisation, as well as other problems, to be worked out by His Church. We are willing to argue the question on the ground of expediency, and many of us have quite open minds as to whether a modified form of episcopacy might not be grafted with advantage upon the Presbyterian system. As a fact, at the Reformation an order of superintendents was given a place in the Scottish Church, and our Presbyterianism need not be more doctrinaire than that of John Knox. At the same time, we have no reason whatever to offer an apology for our Presbyterian constitution. If appeal he made to antiquity, we can claim the admission of the greatest of recent Anglican scholars that in the apostolic age the names of bishop and presbyter were used indifferently and interchangeably of the same persons. We do not know much about the organisation of the Church in the first century, but we at least know that in the year 100 A.D. the Church in Rome was practically Presbyterian. If the test be expediency, there are no doubt great apparent advantages in the Episcopal system—founding, as it does, on the fact that ministers are not equal by nature or grace, that some are born to lead, and some to follow, and that in all other fields of work there emerge various grades of service and honour. But, on the other hand, it is matter of common remark that the main body of our Presbyterian clergy exhibit an unusually high average of learning, individuality, and force of character; and this may well be traceable to the fact that a unique trust was placed in them, and that unique responsibilities were imposed upon them, under our system of ministerial parity. What I am more certain of is, that one effect of our constitution,

which was to give to laymen a recognised place, and
an effective voice, in the courts of the Church, had
not a little to do with developing on the part
of our people a measure of devotion, liberality, and
voluntary service of which any Church in the world
would be proud, which few have equalled, and none
have eclipsed.

II.

THE GOSPEL IN THE PRESBYTERIAN SETTING.

But it is not its type of ecclesiastical constitution,
and its theory of the ministry, that have given Presbyterianism its place in history. These only fashioned
a piece of organisation; and organisation only directs
and applies power. To create power needs a gospel;
and Presbyterianism was served heir to a heart-
compelling and will-subduing gospel. This was the
gospel of the redemption of the world through Jesus
Christ, and of a salvation appropriated by faith,
which had been rediscovered in the Protestant
Reformation, which, after being preached by Luther,
was cast in the moulds of Calvin's thought, and
which was embodied by John Knox in the Scots
Confession. It is true that the name of John Calvin
is no longer one to conjure with. Many of his tenets
provoke the modern mind to protest—especially his
doctrine of particular election and reprobation. But
let us do justice to his system as a whole—to the
scheme of evangelical Christianity which lay at the

heart of it, and to its effect in building for human souls a spiritual dwelling-place which was richly charged with the sanctities, the solemnities, and the responsibilities of existence. From him Presbyterianism took over a gospel of individual salvation in which human souls found peace with God, deliverance from the guilt and from the power of sin, strength for the hour of temptation and trial, light and comfort in the valley of the shadow; and to him also it owed the vision of a Kingdom of God which earnest men should take a hand in building in the midst of human society and on the solid earth, to the end that God's will may be done in earth as it is in heaven.

III.

PRESBYTERIAN WORSHIP.

Another notable feature of Presbyterianism was the simplicity and spirituality of its public worship. It was based on the principle that the staple of the worship called divine service should consist of God's word to man and of man's word to God, and that everything should be ruled out from the Church fabric as well as from the service which was of human invention, or which might distract the mind from attentive hearing or heart-felt worship of Almighty God. In recent years, no doubt, Presbyterianism has departed widely from the ideas of our forefathers as to purity of worship by laying the Fine Arts under contribution to beautify the sanctuary—making use of instrumental music, and embellishing the house of God with the paintings and sculptures which were formerly abhorred as painted or graven images. But the true genius of Presbyterianism is not tied to stereotyped forms, and I do not believe that in the modern reaction we have violated any important principle. The changes can be defended on the ground that the house of God is worthy of our best offerings, and that while there was a danger in the old days that images, painted or sculptured, might lead to idolatry, this danger has ceased to exist in view of the temper and the habits of the modern mind. We do not violate the Presbyterian tradition by making our services more reverent and dignified, though we shall break with it to our loss if we forget that Presbyterianism has ever flourished through the preaching of the Word.

IV.

PRESBYTERIANISM AS A NATIONAL TRADITION.

It is a weighty element in the power of Presbyterianism that it has behind it a great national tradition. The attachment of the Scottish people to the Presbyterian Church is due in no small measure to the fact that in its origin and history it is bound up with inspiring memories of heroism in action and suffering. Few modern men make the same impression of power as John Knox, the Haddington peasant, who bore him-

self as an Old Testament prophet among kings and
courtiers, and changed the whole current, political
as well as religious, of the national life. We also
possess the Covenanters, who claimed liberty to
serve God according to conscience, and who were
shot down and gibbeted and exiled in tens of
thousands for their stand against tyranny. At a
later date, in an age when material interests seemed
to be gaining the upper hand, there came the impressive event of the Disruption, in which many good
men made a great renunciation in defence of the
freedom of the Church which they held to be menaced,
and of the rights of Christ which they held to be
infringed. At some stages of the history there may
be room for doubt as to how far martyrdom was a
necessary form of testimony, but it stands out palpably
from the whole story that (to use a phrase of Dr. Dykes)
Calvinistic Presbyterianism put iron into the blood of
the race, and nerved it to do and to dare things which
were to be an abiding inspiration to the after-world.
Scottish Presbyterianism has believed so strongly in
the sovereignty of God, and in the civil magistrate as
the representative of God on earth for the restraint and
punishment of wickedness, that it has ever shown scant
sympathy with the interpretation of Christian principles which is attempted from the Quaker standpoint.
The peculiar Scottish combination of spiritual religion
with patriotic fervour has been transmitted to the
Colonies, from which it is reported that the membership of the Presbyterian Churches has made an

extraordinary response to the call of the war. It is also noteworthy that, notwithstanding the spirituality of their ministerial tradition, the Scottish Churches have set free a number even of their ordained ministers for combatant service in the present conflict. Upon the merits of this controversy I shall not enlarge, except to say that, while it may be strongly argued that ministerial service is so needful to national well-being that it is inexpedient to withdraw ministers from the spiritual sphere, it is extremely difficult to lay down a principle which demands the immunity of the clergy from military service in a just war. The Druid priests of ancient Gaul had some principle which they could state as dictated by a pagan conception of sanctity; the Roman Catholic Church founds its main objection on the doctrine of transubstantiation; but those who are neither pagans nor Roman Catholics do not find it easy to explain why an office should be so holy as to preclude its occupant from taking direct part in a holy war. If the Quaker attitude is the ideal for the clergy, it is not easy to explain why it is not the ideal for all other Christians.

V.

SOME CHURCH PRINCIPLES.

Presbyterianism is not a hide-bound and unchanging system. It has changed in many ways from time to time. It has been in its day a revolutionary factor, and it has now the reputation of being one of the conservative and steadying forces in political societies. We do not distantly recognise ourselves in the Presbyterian portrait as painted by Dryden and the author of *Hudibras*. It was once thought to be a synonym for bigotry, and to-day it exhibits a breadth and toleration in ecclesiastical matters in comparison with which the attitude of Churches which arrogate to themselves the name of Catholic might seem to an outsider to be properly described as sectarian. And it has developed a new spirit in the matter of union. During more than a century it might seem that it was destined to endless division and subdivision, and those of our countrymen who emigrated to the States and the Colonies might be seen perpetuating our minutest subdivisions, and even refusing to hold communion with other Presbyterians who differed from them on some minor points of polity or worship. With the nineteenth century the tide turned, and there began a process of reconsolidation which in the homeland first gathered up a number of smaller denominations into the United Presbyterian Church, and which was carried further in the fusion of that Church with the Church of the Disruption into the United Free Church of Scotland. In Australia and Canada the project has been mooted, and meets with general favour, of seeking a wider synthesis by the union of the Presbyterian Church with the Methodist and Congregational bodies. At home the same tendency, which the secular mind would call the spirit of the age, and in which we recognise the mind of our

Master and the leading of the Holy Ghost, has pressed upon us the question whether the time has not come to attempt to surmount the obstacles which separate us, and to combine the material and spiritual resources of the two great divisions of Scottish Presbyterianism in a reunited Church of Scotland.

1 do not intend to enter fully into a discussion of the policy which has been proposed as a basis of union. The leading idea of that policy is that the path to union lies in reconciling and combining two principles which have made up a large part of the history of Scottish Presbyterianism, and which are held by the two Churches in common, but with the practical application of which they have been identified in different and special ways. The United Free Church has magnified the principle of spiritual freedom : we recognise that it will not enter into a union which would compromise its past attitude, and we are prepared to take the necessary steps to ensure that its convictions on the subject will be respected in the constitution of a reunited Church. On the other hand, it is not open to doubt that from the Reformation down to recent times it was the overwhelming desire of the Scottish people that the Presbyterian Church should have the aspect, not only of a branch of the Church of Christ, but also of a national institution—serving as an organ of national testimony to the national faith, and also of a spiritual service co-extensive with the needs of Scotland ; this tradition is enshrined in the heart of the Church of which I am a minister ; and it has to be recognised

with equal frankness that on our side there will be no consent to a breach with this tradition which would commit the State to a position of ostentatious neutrality towards the faith and the Church of the Scottish people, and which would divert its ancient patrimony to secular uses.   We believe that we can meet—and please God we shall meet—those who say that it is indispensable that we should enter into a larger freedom as the condition of union, and we are hopeful that they will also be prepared to meet us on the ground of conserving in substance the traditional Scottish form of the national recognition of religion.

VI.

THE PRESBYTERIAN CHARACTER.

There is another and homelier test of the value of a Church, and that is its average output—the quality of the typical men and women whom it moulds from generation to generation.   It may well increase our respect for the Church in general that it is one of the few agencies in the world that are able to make upon character a deep and abiding mark for good.   There is a recognisable type of character, with well-marked virtues and equally noticeable limitations, which is associated with each of the great historic Churches of Christendom; and Presbyterianism has been able on the whole to affix a very distinct and a more than respectable hall-mark of its own.   Not the least ground of my own belief in Presbyterianism is the respect and affection which I have felt for those men and women who seemed to be the typical representatives of its piety and virtue. This is the general picture of them as I have known them—diligent in business, truthful in word, upright in deed, cautious and moderate in their judgment, though with a reserve power of dogged determination and of moral indignation, clean in heart and mind, loyal to friend and to principles, reticent in religion but possessed withal by the fear of God, by a deep reverence for divine things, by a warm attachment to the Church visible, and by a courageous faith in the gospel of Christ and the life of the world to come. We have also had our special type of womanhood, which at its best had hardly its equal in intellectual vigour, and certainly not its superior in unselfish and self-sacrificing devotion. No doubt there were defects, even serious defects, in the traditional type of Scottish character. There was a considerable legacy from the natural man—a spirit of combativeness, a strain of narrowness, a sturdy assertion of the claims of self, a vein of coarseness, while the Christian qualities showed some deficiency on the side of the special graces of the New Testament code. But all in all the tradition of Scottish character is a rich inheritance and a worthy inspiration, which was the result of a real leavening and moulding of human nature by the power of the Holy Ghost. Those who are interested in the point have shown that the Church of Scotland can make out as plausible a claim as any other Church to a lineal descent of our ministry from the apostles, but for my part I find the virtues and graces of the inner circle of our people to be sufficient credentials of a true branch of the Church of Christ.   May we have grace, when seeking for more goodly pearls of the Kingdom, to keep those which we have inherited.   Amen.

XI

REVERENCE.

"Put off thy shoes from off thy feet, for the place whereon thou standest is holy ground."—EXODUS iii. 5.

THE subject of this sermon is Reverence—its nature, its objects, and the ways in which it may be instilled and fostered. A good reason for taking up the subject is that on the one hand it has been agreed by many earnest thinkers that it is one of the most essential, as well as one of the fairest, of the graces of the human spirit, while, on the other hand, there is a widespread impression that the decay of reverence is one of the most marked and regrettable features of the life of the age in which we live.

Very noteworthy, to begin with, is the unanimity with which the gifted writers of last century accorded to reverence a high place, and almost the highest place, in the holy family of the virtues and the graces. In a well-known passage in *Wilhelm Meister*, Goethe declared reverence to be the essence even of religion. He said that there have been three types of religion in the world—paganism, which reveres as divine the universe around us; the Old Testament religion, which lifted its eyes to the God in heaven above; and Christianity, which adores God as revealed in the humiliation and suffering of the Man of Sorrows. This conception was taken over by Carlyle, who, with characteristic heat and iteration, insisted on "the indispensableness of reverence," and insisted on it the more because in the form which it assumes in hero-worship—in loyalty and obedience to the great man—he saw the only hope of making much of the stumbling hordes of our weak and foolish world. Ruskin preached it as unweariedly as Carlyle, while practising the virtue more consistently. Similarly Tennyson:

> "Let knowledge grow from more to more,
>   But more of reverence in us dwell;
>   That mind and soul, according well,
> May make one music as before."

And this estimate of the importance of reverence was shared by our philosophers. Martineau describes it as "the apex and crown of character." "If with all your learning," said our greatest Scottish educationist in an address to teachers, "you have failed to evoke reverence, you have failed altogether."

It is true that from the point of view of Scripture this strain of panegyric may seem exaggerated. In the teaching of Scripture some other things are counted more important—as repentance from sin, faith in God the Father and the Lord Jesus Christ, obedience to the holy and righteous will of God. If there were not other and higher standards we might well suppose, after witnessing a Mussulman at prayer, that there was more true religion in a Mohammedan mosque than in a Presbyterian church. But, while reverence is certainly not the be-all and the end-all of religion, it appears in Scripture as an indispensable symptom and accompaniment of true religion. Religion, when it is a heartfelt reality, necessarily shapes for itself a ritual eloquently expressive of dependence upon God, of penitence, adoration, and trust. In the homage of the bowed head, the closed eyes, and the shoeless feet, in the appeal of the outstretched hands, in the ritual of bodily prostration and the putting on of sackcloth and ashes, the piety of the Old Testament found expression no less picturesque than vehement. In his vision of the heavenly sanctuary Isaiah saw the Seraphim veiling their faces with their wings as they rendered to the Eternal their ceaseless anthem of praise: "Holy, Holy, Holy is the Lord God of Hosts." We may also recall how Jesus Christ inculcated and practised a deep reverence for God's name and His works, when He bade us to swear neither by His throne nor by His footstool; for His Word, which He warned us against making of none effect by our traditions; for His house, which He cleansed of an unholy traffic; for the image of God in man, which He discovered even in the most insignificant, degraded, and wretched of the children of Adam, and because of which He taught us to attach to the individual soul a value exceeding that of all the material wealth of a world.

I.

THE VALUE OF REVERENCE.

Why, now, has so great importance been attached to this grace of reverence? The reasons, I think, are two—one, that it is a symptom of a noble type of character, and the other that it helps to mould a noble type of character.

1. Reverence is a revelation of the finer type of soul. It means that one bears oneself in a seemly and worthy manner among the great things of existence and the sanctities of human life. It is also evidence of a becoming humility of spirit. The reverent man is one who shows in his bearing that he is above the vulgar illusion which makes self the centre of his universe, and that he has a tolerably clear apprehension of his humbler place in the scheme and scale of things, and of his standing in the court of duty and in the presence of God. Moreover, the fact that a man reverences what is great and good in others is evidence that his own character contains at least the germs of the same excellences, while contrariwise, the man who reveres nothing and nobody arouses a strong presumption that there is little in himself which entitles him even to respect.

2. Reverence also helps to make a noble character. It involves the desire to become like to, or at least to be closely associated with, the objects that have impressed us. If we truly revere God, Jesus

taught, we shall seek to become like Him in the bounti-
fulness of His love, and in His readiness to forgive.
The true adoration of Christ, as we read in passages
in the New Testament, issues in our being changed
into His image from glory to glory.   The value of
the form of reverence known as hero-worship lies in
the fact that it disposes us to imitate those who
are better and wiser than ourselves, or at least
to ask to be used in doing their greater work and in
carrying out their larger plans.

II.

THE MODERN DECAY OF REVERENCE.

The strong insistence on reverence by the great
writers to whom I have referred was due to the fact
that they found much evidence of the growth of a
spirit of irreverence in the modern world.   This
decay of reverence was noted and lamented throughout the whole English-speaking world, and we may
note some of the forms in which it was chiefly
manifested.

1. To begin with, there has been a marked change in
the relations of what the Catechism calls superiors and
inferiors.   We have witnessed a general uprising of the
inferior.   One of the most noticeable features of family
life in recent times is the self-assertion of children,
who at the best offer their parents affection rather
than reverence.   It is a common remark of middle-

aged people that they would never have dared to address their parents in the way in which their children speak to them. The mistress of a household feels that authority over her servants depends almost entirely upon her own capacity and force of character, and derives little extraneous support from the superiority of her office. In earlier times the common mind was much impressed by the apostolic injunction not "to speak evil of dignities"—which was interpreted to mean that every one in a public station, from the King on the throne to the magnate of a parish, was to be protected from malicious and contemptuous criticism by the dignity of his position. To-day there is a vast number of people whose intellectual luxury is to talk the language of detraction, and perhaps of calumny, about those whom they dislike because of their superiority to themselves, or only because of their greater success in life. The change is, of course, no matter of regret so far as it means that even the greatest must now submit to moral criticism, and also that there is a decay of the spirit which Thackeray satirised in the *Book of Snobs*. But there is still a virtue which lies half-way between irreverence and servility.

2. There is also much irreverent handling of great themes. There has been a rather noticeable change in the general tone as regards the providential order of things, and the sacred and solemn things of human life. The same Catechism bids us to speak reverently of the works of God; and occurrences which were

formerly spoken of with reverence as the acts of God are now treated unthinkingly and habitually as the subject of complaint or jest. The topic of the weather is a significant illustration. Compare with the querulousness of modern talk the rebuke of the Scottish shepherd to one who complained of the persistent rain: "It slockens the ewes, and it's God's will." Experiences of human life, with which are bound up so much of its beauty and pathos, furnish the occasion of an infinite output of frivolous thought and speech. Birth, love, marriage, death, and the domestic relationships, not excluding even the sorrowful case of the widow and the fatherless, are found to have their amusing aspects, and to provoke the witty sallies of the brighter spirits. For this some blame used to be laid at the door of American humorists, whose humour largely consisted in treating the big things of life, as well as the great men of the present and the past, with an offensive familiarity; but the brilliant gifts of Mr. Bernard Shaw have been partly prostituted in the same way, as he himself reminded us by printing a correspondence in which the deep-hearted Tolstoy indignantly refused to have anything more to say to a man who could treat God's universe and human life as a joke, and not even a very good joke. The true humour rather seeks to dignify the commonplace; and it is a spurious sort which tries to amuse us by dragging down the objects which have a right to be handled with veneration and awe.

3. The decay of reverence has also been increasingly apparent in the sphere of holy things, narrowly so-called. As touching God's Day, it is possible to think that there was too much of the Old Testament in our traditional method of Sabbath-observance, and at the same time to hold that it is an irreparable loss when the Sunday ceases to be observed as a day dedicated to worship, to serious reading and reflection, and to works of mercy. The Word of God, when it is not treated with the utter neglect which is the extreme of irreverence, is often made use of in a way that would have shocked the piety of an earlier age. The Biblical text or incident, which formerly was quoted only in serious religious discussion or in the ministry of the sick-room, is now freely used to light up a political argument, or to give piquancy to a repartee. In bygone times countless lives have been touched to abiding seriousness, and imbued with the deepest sense of moral responsibility, by the well-founded doctrine of a future state of retribution; to-day, if we open the latest collection of good stories we might conclude that for the modern mind Hell hardly exists, save for the opportunity which it gives for pointing a grim joke. As touching God Himself, it will hardly be disputed that there has been a general weakening of the sense of the presence and rule of the Almighty which was a characteristic note of the religion of earlier days, and that few draw near to Him with the reverence and godly fear that beseems

the finite and sinful creature in making the approach to an infinite and all-holy God.

4. Something might be also said of the causes which have led to the modern decay of reverence. Two especially have been dwelt upon as explaining, if not extenuating, the defect. One is that the modern world has found out and accomplished so many wonderful things that it has become somewhat conceited, and vanity is ever disposed to be patronising and even contemptuous rather than reverent. Something is also due to a weakening of religious faith. But perhaps the chief reason is that we require leisure in order to allow great objects to make their due impression upon the mind; and the strain and worry of modern life leave many with little time in which to think about aught save the pressing concerns of the passing day, and to gain the elevation of mind which results from wide prospects.

III.

A REVIVAL OF REVERENCE.

The human spirit is very complex, and there is another side which must in fairness be recognised, and which even shows in certain fields a growth and deepening of reverence. And in the first place it may be remarked that there is an irreverence which may be only superficial and formal—somewhat of the nature of "inverted hypocrisy." The flippancy

with which the younger generation was colourably
credited had a good deal of this character. It was
often said in the days before the earthquake that the
grave, earnest mood of our Scottish forefathers had
been replaced by a spirit which played at life and
only took games seriously; and to-day we feel that
the grandfathers who solemnly spoke of the ensnaring
temptations of the world, and extracted from the
world a large measure of profit and comfort, did not
front the great issues of life with more fundamental
seriousness than their grandsons who, perhaps with a
jest on their lips, faced the worst terrors that the
world can marshal in simple obedience to the call
of duty. To take a concrete case, it seemed a climax
of irreverence when a battalion, charging through a
murderous fire, drove a football towards the enemy's
trenches, but it has to be taken along with the fact
that the same men were sacrificing in a cause which
they deemed sacred all that human nature holds dear,
and also that many had humbly commended their souls
to God before they went over the parapet. The Scottish
mind has always understood, when left to its own
instincts, that there may be smiling ripples on the
ocean of the solemnities.

1. More specially, there has been witnessed, apart
from the temporary check of the war, a growing
reverence for man as man. It was said that
one of the most distinctive features of our Lord's
teaching was that He emphasised the unique dignity
and immeasurable value of the soul of man as a being

made in the image of God, and this has entered deeply into our modern thinking. A profound reverence for human life, a high estimate of the value of all that appears in human form, underlies the extraordinary zeal and energy which have been directed in recent times to the relief of the sick, the infirm, the aged, and even of the insane and the criminal. It may seem to a brutal common-sense that there is a great mass of human beings whose life is worthless, which it is foolish to seek to preserve, and which might well be allowed to sink out of existence under its weakness and woes; but we have learned so much in the school of Christ that we judge human nature, even when ruined by disease or vice, to be majestic in its ruins, and we hardly think any price too high to pay to rescue a single life from death, and we gladly extend relief and succour to the most bruised, maimed, and seemingly useless of the beings who are made in the likeness of man. It may also well be thought to be a remarkable proof of the influence of Christ that, while by nature we look on the lower races of the human as almost a different species, and upon the lowest as on a level with the brute creation, the Church has built up a great spiritual enterprise which rests upon a belief in the unity of the human race and the brotherhood of man, and upon a reverential regard for even the most uncivilised and degraded as children of the same Heavenly Father with ourselves, redeemed by the same Saviour, and destined to the same inheritance.

2. Another striking fact, of similar character, is the growing reverence which is felt for childhood. I have said that children do not seem to revere their parents as in former days, but there is an offset to this in the fact that parents now show much more reverence for their children. More and more we are found reverently dwelling upon the spell and the claims of childhood. It is not only that we feel, in Wordsworth's phrase, that "Heaven lies about them in their infancy"—that being nearer to the source of infinite purity they have around them something of a heavenly purity and brightness: rather it is that, amid the imperfections and failures of later life, there is a deep realisation of the immeasurable possibilities that open out before the young, an earnest desire that avoiding our sins they may escape the punishments which followed, and a prayer and a hope that they may be guided and used as instruments in bringing in a better and brighter day in our old sad world.

IV.

THE CULTURE OF REVERENCE.

I conclude this subject with some remarks on the culture and conservation of the grace of reverence.

1. It is generally agreed that for the instilment of reverence much depends on the character of those with whom, in the formative period of life, a child is

brought in contact. It is in reverence for parents and teachers that the culture naturally begins, and those are unfortunate indeed who did not discover in their home life the objects that draw out the instinctive capacity for reverence. This point was strikingly put by Carlyle in a reference to the influences of his own childhood, " The highest whom I knew on earth I saw bowed down with awe unspeakable before a higher in Heaven. Such things, especially in infancy, reach inwards to the very core of your being; mysteriously does a Holy of Holies build itself into visibility in the mysterious deeps; and reverence, the divinest in man, springs undying from its mean envelopment of fear."

2. In the second place it should be pointed out that for the culture of the spirit of reverence no small importance attaches to outward acts. In the book already referred to the wise Goethe taught that if children are to imbibe the spirit it ought to be expressed in attitudes, postures, and gestures which symbolise the attitude of the reverent soul towards the universe around us, and to the God who has been revealed to us in exaltation and humiliation. The reverent action, when it has become habitual, is a constant summons to reverence of soul. This has also been commonly recognised by the Churches. It is a reproach which, not without some ground, has been brought against Presbyterianism, that it has been too indifferent to training the young to the outward forms of reverence in worship and in daily

life; and while this had formerly some defence in the theory that where true piety is engendered the forms of reverence may be expected to reproduce themselves spontaneously, it must be granted that we have something to learn from other communions in the aid to religion which is supplied in the habitual practice of reverent bearing and devotional act.

3. And lastly, let us remember that the grand object, and also the enduring spring of reverential feeling, is God. It is God that the child is instinctively·seeking in its quest for something perfectly wise and great and good among the broken lights of earth. Moreover, it is at least the rule that the spirit of reverence endures amid the trying experiences of later life only if our souls be rooted in faith in God. For human experience is to some extent a process of disenchantment in regard to those who were idealised and glorified by the optimism and faith of youth. The imperfections of our nearest are painfully, if unwillingly, realised. We outgrow many of our early heroes, we are disappointed in many of our friends. It is impressively borne in upon us that in human nature there is not only a spark of divinity, but a large bulk of common clay; and it is not easy, unless we truly believe in the Being in whom is all perfection, for us to be saved from the doubt and mistrust which give birth to a general spirit of scepticism and cynicism. The great need of our minds is so to realise God—the Almighty,

the All-wise, the All-good—that He supplies a
permanent factor in all our serious thinking, a sacred
vein in our deepest feeling, and a powerful incentive
in all deliberate and weighty actions.   And because
it is difficult for us to apprehend Him in His
transcendence and His infinitude, He has drawn near
to us in Jesus Christ—so that we can behold His
glory in the face of one like to ourselves, can believe
that he that hath seen Him hath seen the Father,
and may be drawn by His word and His grace into
the experience of the life of God.   Amen.

XII.

SPOTS ON THE LOVE-FEASTS.

"These are spots in your feasts of charity."—JUDE 12.
"But as for me and my house, we will serve the Lord."—
JOSHUA xxiv. 15.

THE Feast of Charity was an institution of the primitive Church that shows how much it was in earnest with the principle of Christian brotherhood. The early Christians considered it as natural that the members of a congregation should meet for a common meal as that they should meet for common worship. Hence arose the Love-feast—a congregational dinner or supper which was probably a weekly event, and which was followed and hallowed by the celebration of the Holy Communion. It has even been argued that in the early period this common meal was identical with the Communion service. By many ancient writers the Love-feast was warmly extolled. "It is a truly Christlike institution," they said, "for it fosters brotherly love, inculcates humility, and relieves and solaces poverty." So popular was the institution that when the great St. Augustine, four centuries after our era, attempted to put it down in his African diocese, he tells us that riots broke out, and that he was even in some danger of his life.

Beautiful, however, as was the Love-feast in expressing the sentiment of brotherhood, and useful as it was in linking religion to social life, it soon developed certain objectionable features. Unworthy guests found their way to the table — attracted thither, not by the communion of saints, but by the loaves, the fishes, and the wine; and the scandalous spectacle was seen of men eating and drinking to excess, and then taking into their polluted hands the sacred emblems of the body and blood of the Lord. Others, we read, disdained to eat of the common provision, and brought with them luxuries for their own exclusive enjoyment. Again, there were those who did not respect the devotional aims of the gathering, but gave utterance to heretical or revolutionary opinions, and thus aroused theological or political passions. By these and other abuses, it was felt, the Love-feast was being spoiled; in our text the writer deplores them or the people responsible for them as "spots in the feasts of charity."

Partly because of the abuses which developed, partly because congregations became too large and unwieldy, the Love-feast eventually disappeared from Church life. In recent times the spirit of the old institution has reappeared to some extent in the attempt to foster the social side of congregational

life; and we may well welcome and support all
agencies and activities which give fuller and clearer
expression to the idea that the Christian society has
the character of a family and household. At the
same time it is evident that the tie constituted by
Church membership cannot, even in the most living
and hearty congregation, yield all that was looked
for from the ancient Love-feast. With the expansion
of the Church and of its congregations it was
inevitable that the place of the Love-feast should
more and more be taken by the Christian family. It
is only in the home that the close and sustained
intimacy which was aimed at in the apostolic
institution continues to be practicable. The home
with its family-table as a daily meeting-ground; with
the intimate association of its members, for years or
for life, on the footing of husband or wife, parent or
child, brother or sister; with its bond of common
interests, common joys, and common sorrows—carries
with it possibilities of influencing and of being
influenced which no other institution can pretend to
rival. The Love-feast instituted by the Church was
more ambitious in its scope and wider in its embrace,
but it could only be a shadow of the Feast of
Charity which has been instituted at our own tables
and around our own hearths.

The home-life the permanent Love-feast is, then,
our subject; and I go on to mention some of the spots
which commonly mar its beauty and dim its lustre.

1. EVASION OF PARENTAL RESPONSIBILITY.—One

might begin by referring to a fundamental heresy which is spreading in the modern world, and which is fraught with the gravest danger to the interests of civilisation and morality. This is the doctrine that the possession of a family is not to be reckoned as a good at all, and to count as an element in human well-being and happiness. We have been so much influenced by the modern novel, which very properly commends marriages of pure affection, that we are apt to forget that it is not wholly a matter of sentiment, and that the normal man owes to society the duty of marrying and rearing children. We shall take it for granted—in accordance with the general tradition of the human race, and the teachings of Scripture—that it is the purpose of God to set us in families as a flock, that children are a blessing, that the home in which children grow up is unequalled as a school of character, and that the relationships of the home have an interest and a value for which no compensation is to be found in any increase of wealth or of individual comfort.

2. ANARCHY IN THE HOME. — Leaving now this unnatural and dangerous theory, we may notice, next, a blemish of family life which transgresses against the essential condition of every form of organised society. It is a familiar saying that order is the first law of God, and of the spots on the Love-feast none is more ominous than that which we may describe as anarchy. By this I mean absence of government—the failure of the responsible head to exercise effective rule over

the subjects. The supreme authority no doubt varies in families as it does in states. The constitution is sometimes of the nature of a monarchy, sometimes of an aristocracy, or even a republic. But some controlling power there ought to be which organises the little commonwealth, frames and enforces its laws, maintains order, and in general determines the character, spirit, and tone of the family. Just as a good newspaper or magazine, though depending on many contributors, possesses an individuality which reflects that of a controlling mind, so the well-ordered family, though including wide differences of temperament, and even of personal conviction, will exhibit a collective character which is a kind of extended personality of its head. It seems, now, to be matter of general observation that throughout the English-speaking world there has been a growing disposition to shirk the responsibilities of government which are laid even by the law of nature upon the heads of families. In this respect a great change has taken place in this country within living memory. In former days the head of a household took his responsibilities so seriously that his rule often passed over into a tyranny; his modern successor often takes his so lightly that he is regarded by his children as a negligible quantity. The old theory was that a father was a being who was to be regarded with awe as the representative of God within his little mundane sphere; now it is not uncommon for him to desire to be regarded by them as merely a good-natured play-

mate and a well-disposed counsellor, whose advice children are free to take or to disregard.   Not that the
traditional system of parental rule was perfect in its
ideal, or wholly good in its results.   It was sometimes
a pure despotism, which crushed the spirit and soured
the temper, and provoked a recoil—when the restraints
were withdrawn—into rebellion against all conven-
tions, and even into sinful license.   And on the other
hand it is clearly a gain that, in the newer practice,
an attempt is made to reduce the aloofness of parent
and child, and to temper the sternness of the relationship by importing into it something of the warmth
and of the confidence of friendship.   At the same
time the older tradition was based on a principle which
lies at the very foundation of family life, and which,
even when exemplified in extreme forms, was far less
dangerous than the total abnegation of parental responsibility—the principle, namely, that it is the
business of the head of a family to rule, to exact
reverence from his subjects, and to embrace their
developing characters and lives within a system of
directing and restraining law, and within the operation of retributive justice.

3. THE EXCESS OF INDIVIDUALISM.—A kindred
blemish, for which it would be unjust to lay all the
blame on the head of the family, is that which may
be described as an excessive individualism.   The time
comes, in the history of a family, when the responsibilities are so far devolved on the whole body, and
the subordinate members are called on to share in

developing a collective life marked by growing richness, beauty, and strength. In many cases they respond very poorly to this appeal. It often happens that the members of the circle have as individuals a sufficient stock of culture and of the virtues, and lead separate lives which are reputable and useful; but they do not co-operate in and contribute to a general life which comes near to representing the wealth and variety of their several resources. Such a family resembles a man who complains that, while he is assured by the doctor that every organ is sound, he has a general feeling of illness and depression. This undue individualism that I speak of is somewhat common among the men, if not among the women, of the race which I know best; and we have perhaps to look to other peoples and other lands for frequent illustrations of the type of family which may be said to have a common mind and heart, in which each member seeks to enrich the whole, and which fosters a common life by carefully cherishing the family customs and institutions. Certain it is that there are families among us the members of which are little more than strangers to one another. Nor is the person at all uncommon who is at his best among strangers, at his worst in the home circle—abroad full of charm and courtesy, at home silent and even morose. It may be added that it is one of the surest tests of true refinement when the members of a family habitually treat one another with rather more respect and consideration than they show to strangers whose good opinion they wish to deserve. "Do not treat a friend," said Hesiod, "quite as if he were a brother." The standard of friendship might with advantage be brought into many of our homes.

4. THE LOVELESS HOME.—A darker spot on the Love-feast is the want of natural affection. This is indeed the fatal blemish, for a home without love is like a body from which the spirit has fled, or like a world without a sun to supply it with light and heat. It is true that appearances are often deceptive in regard to the presence or absence of family affection. There is the discordant home, familiar to many, in which the bells seem to be ever jangled and out of tune, in which a storm is usually either blowing or brewing, in which strife and wrath alternate with moods of sincere contrition and words and acts of reparation. Under the surface of the life of the quarrelsome family, however, there is often a great deep of genuine affection. The same holds of other homes in which there is much appearance of coldness and indifference. Some are so ashamed of any display of feeling that they are misunderstood, not only by others, but by themselves, and often they only find out how strong and tender were the ties which bound them to their kin when these have been ruptured by separation or death. On the other hand, there are homes enough in which there is some public show of affection, but from which the reality has fled. The evil of which I am speaking may come to expression in the negative form of indifference and

neglect.   Or it may take the positive form of active hostility, illustrated by the feud in the family, which is due sometimes to deep-seated differences of temperament, sometimes to collision of opinion on the great issues of religion and politics, sometimes to a parent's favouritism, sometimes to a sense of wrong in the matter of the division of the inheritance.   When relatives have no affection for one another, it may seem idle to exhort them to love one another, since the heart does not readily act at the bidding of the will; but as a fact it is a law of human nature that if we speak kindly words and do kindly deeds—and as much at least as this is always in our power—the affectionate feelings are likely to spring up in their train.   As regards the family feud, it is an old observation that none can hate so bitterly when they fall out as those who were formed by nature to love one another, and before a breach becomes irreparable one should be prepared to make almost any sacrifice that may be needed to remove a sense of injury, and to avert a scandal that may develop into a moral tragedy.

5. INCONSTANCY OF AFFECTION.—As a special form of the last-named defect we may notice inconstancy of affection.   It is saddening to observe how often upon a love that was once real and deep there supervenes estrangement and indifference.   Time, it is true, brings about inward as well as outward changes, and it is foolish to ignore the necessary consequences of the rise of new interests, and the

formation of new ties; but there should ever be preserved in the heart a spirit of loyalty to the sacred bonds and associations of the past. Nothing but death — and not even death — should wholly sunder the spiritual bonds of family life. Of parental love, at least, we expect that it will endure to the end. It seems to be a law of the animal creation that affection lasts only so long as the young require protection and sustenance; but men and women were made to embody a different idea of the Creator. It was not intended that a father should close his door in implacable wrath against a prodigal son; or that a mother's devotion should pass into coldness or even dislike towards a daughter when she has grown into a woman with an independent mind and will, and a life which she herself was given responsibility to make or mar. It must, however, be said that the decay of parental affection is a much less noticeable fact than the inability of children to realise the sacrifices that were made for them by their parents, and their failure to make to them a due return in affection and gratitude. There are many people in the Colonies who have parents that took the trouble to rear them in the old country and to launch them in the world, and who on their part hardly take the trouble to write them a letter to let them know that they are alive and how they are faring. It is probable, indeed, that such neglect is not very common when there is anything creditable to report; but we can readily think of many other, though less heinous, breaches of the law that, having loved our own, we should love them to the end. It may be added that, though our race has a proverb that blood is thicker than water, there are few of us who sufficiently think of these two things—one the magnitude of the debt a child owes to a good mother, which it is impossible ever adequately to acknowledge and repay; the other the right which the member of a family has to expect at the hands of a brother or a sister the charity that never faileth—even the love " that beareth all things, that believeth all things, that hopeth all things, that endureth all things."

6. THE DISHONOURED HOME.—There is another spot on the Love-feast that may hardly be passed over —the stain on the good name of the family. Many have a cross of this kind, and often a heavy cross, to bear. In our time of restless movement, when so many are torn away early from steadying and re-straining influences, there are homes enough in which there is mourning over a prodigal son who died in the midst of his days, or who lingered on in disgrace. It is a more crushing blow when the humiliation comes through one of the heads of the family—when a father or a mother, whom God meant to stand to the children as the representatives of wisdom, strength, and goodness, and to be reverenced accordingly, is discovered to be adjudged by society as a disreputable person, and causes them to hang their heads in shame. It is doubly tragic because the children sometimes fail to surmount the disadvantages which were en-

tailed upon them by a bad ancestry and a dishonoured name, and the grim saying of the Hebrews is illustrated afresh—that "the fathers ate sour grapes and the children's teeth were set on edge." On the other hand, it is observable that this worst of calamities is sometimes overruled for good in the after-history of a family. Some of the most earnest of social workers came from homes upon which there lay a shadow of a vice, and, conceiving a deep horror of the evil thing which had darkened the morning of their lives, they threw themselves with extraordinary energy into the battle against the sins that ravage and desolate our world, and chiefly against the vice which had brought to their own loved ones humiliation and sorrow.

7. THE IRRELIGIOUS HOME.—Our list, which is by no means exhaustive, naturally leads up to 'the case of the irreligious family life. It is, of course, unjust to judge of the extent and reality of religion by external forms, but it is at least a somewhat serious matter that in the modern Protestant world family religion seems to have shrunk to smaller visible dimensions than in any previous phase of religious history, and that there is many a respectable family in which it would be difficult for an observer to discover—apart from occasional church attendance—what form of the Christian religion it professed, or if it professed any form at all. There are, in particular, three forms in which family-religion was formerly manifested, and the decay of which gives grave concern to those who believe that the State rests upon the family, and that

the family must rest upon religion. One is family-worship. It would seem that in a household which professes to be Christian the irreducible minimum of family religion would be for the head of the house-hold to read in the family-circle of a Sunday evening a chapter from the Bible, and to ask upon those present and absent, and upon relatives, friends, and country, the blessing of Almighty God. Not only is this a due tribute of homage and gratitude to the Creator, and a proved means of grace, but it is an assertion of the spiritual unity of the family; and in addition to claiming the reward of prayer, it helps to strengthen that unity by the formation of sacred associations which haunt the memory throughout the later life. The family, again, in earlier times served an all-important function as a school of moral and religious instruction; but it is not at all certain that the average modern parent realises that the duty is laid upon him, and cannot be delegated to others, of training his children in the fear of God and in the keeping of His com-mandments, and in warning them against the tempta-tions and the evils that are in the world. And lastly, one discerns a grave danger to the unity and sanctity of family life in the growing disinclination of young men to claim full membership in the Christian Church. In many instances the two generations of fathers and sons are separated, not only by differences of age and of interests, but by the deeper difference which is made by profession and non-profession of the Christian faith. I do not, of course, say that it is the duty of every young man reared in a Christian family to become a communicant in the Christian Church. If a man has broken radically with the faith of his fathers, he is to be commended for his honesty in declining to profess a faith which he does not hold. If, again, while holding the faith of his fathers, he is living a life which is deliberately selfish and worldly, and stained by grievous sin, he is indeed blameworthy for being content to live on so low a level, but also to be commended for not pretending to be a better man than he is in intention and fact. But if he honestly believes the fundamental truths of the Christian religion, and is sincerely minded to live an upright and pure life, he incurs a grave responsibility in refusing to take his place in the Christian Church. Apart from his own personal loss, he sins against the family by interfering in a most important particular with the unity of its life, and by preventing it from appearing as a whole before God, on the holiest ground on earth, with a united voice of profession, thanksgiving, and supplication, and of dedication to the service of God.

In these latter days much is said about the importance of the Church working for social salvation. The idea is not so much of a novelty as is often thought: the Reformed Churches, and also the Roman Catholic Church, have recognised from of old that they had a commission to seek to work out social salvation, and if there be a difference in the matter between the older and the newer British Protestantism it is chiefly that the older generations accomplished much and said little about it, while the present generation talks a great deal about it and has yet to show that its much speaking will be followed by as considerable results. This is illustrated in the history of the family. In former days the Church, without any special organisation and effort, was successful in creating a Christian home which had the atmosphere of a sanctuary, and was also remarkably efficient as a school of character; while at the present day, although there are numerous societies, ecclesiastical, educational, and philanthropic, which discuss and stimulate the life of the family in every possible aspect, they are fairly satisfied when they are able to check deterioration, and to strengthen the good elements that have survived.

At all events, social salvation is a great and a partially realisable ideal; and in the programme of social salvation no item is so vital as that which is concerned with the all-important social unit of the family. The importance of the family for the Church can hardly be exaggerated. The Christian message, to take a preliminary point, needs illumination from the fairer and richer experiences of family life to make it intelligible: the gospel of divine fatherhood depends for its music, the principle of human brotherhood for its ethical appeal, on the associations which for the hearers have already gathered about those names. Further, it is matter of common observation, and has been confirmed by special research into the subject, that a very large proportion of the members, and of the best members of our churches, consists of those who received a Christian nurture in the family, and for whom the home was the forecourt of the temple. A large percentage of those who profess the experience of a conscious conversion ascribe it in the last resort to home influences, and the percentage is very much larger in the case of those who by the path of a gradual conversion have reached the state of grace which is vouched for by transparently Christian character and by character's unmistakable fruits. No less is the welfare of the State dependent upon the extent to which the home rises to the height of its ideal, and serves as the moral and spiritual ally of the school. The failures of education which are so often deplored are traceable in large measure to the failure of the home to support the intellectual training by the supplementary discipline which it should provide, and it is certain that even if we had the best of schools for children of every class we should do no more than hold our ground unless we could also get better homes.

Although there is ground for thinking that the home has recently undergone some deterioration among us, that the spots on the Love-feasts have even multiplied and broadened, there is no reason to take a despondent view. For of all the social spheres the family is that which is by nature most nearly Christian in spirit, life, and aims. It can be said of it with

truth that it is not far from the kingdom of God.   It
reflects in its constitution what we believe to be the
system and the order which exist within the Godhead
itself.   In its life, connected as it is with the
impressive events of birth and death, piety is instinctive and spontaneous, and easy to cultivate.
Within its borders self is less clamant than in other
compartments of our existence, and love, even self-
sacrificing love, very readily asserts its rights and its
privileges.   Very powerful, therefore, are the spiritual
auxiliaries which join hands with those who labour
so to build it and furnish it that the glory of the
later temple may be greater than the glory of the
first, and that it may do what God expected of it in
the extension of His Kingdom.   Amen.

XIII.

THE SOCIAL MISSION OF THE CHURCH.

"Neighbour unto him that fell among the thieves."—LUKE x. 36.

THE peculiarity of our age and country is not that social misery is more rife than formerly, but that we realise it more vividly and discuss it more freely. One reason is that we live in an age which delights in research and statistics. Another reason, let us hope, is that the general conscience has grown more sensitive. And yet again, we have made such extraordinary progress in other directions that we cannot fail to be deeply impressed by the failures which stand out in contrast to the triumphs of modern civilisation.

In truth, the contrasts which are presented by modern society are nothing less than sensational, and Scotland has its full share of them. Could one of our forefathers, familiar with the poverty and other distresses of our dark ages, revisit the Scotland of to-day, he would be lost in astonishment. He would congratulate us on our long immunity from the horrors of invasion and civil war, on the transformation of a country of half-starved peasants into a busy and rich hive of industry, on a universal system of education which was a door of entrance into the realms of knowledge and culture, and on the secure position of civil and religious liberties. It would appear to him in short that most of the things which men fought for in the old time, and others which they hardly dared to pray for, had actually come to pass. But as he pursued his investigations, he would find out that there was much to confirm the old suspicion that every fulfilment of a great hope carries with it a great disappointment. At the heart of this imposing civilisation, with its victorious industry and its accumulation of wealth, he would find men begging for work and children crying for bread. In the great cities with their stately public buildings and their luxurious dwellings, their institutions dedicated to the luxuries of art and amusement, their promenades ablaze with the pride of life, he would find districts in which families were huddled together in indescribable squalor, and a prepared soil that brought forth its abundant and manifold fruits of vice and crime.

We cannot here attempt to analyse the various causes which, in conjunction with ingrained tendencies, are responsible for the material misery and the moral degradation that prevail in our midst. It may, however, be pointed out that the evils are intimately connected with the revolution in the methods of production which was carried out during the eighteenth and nineteenth centuries, and which transformed the little peasant-state into an important industrial and commercial country. This change was accompanied by a wide displacement and also by a vast increase of the population, which flocked to the new labour-market in the factory, the mine, or the shipbuilding yard, and, as it multiplied, converted villages into towns, and towns into cities, and added to the nucleus of the old cities, which in some cases had decayed into slums, their spreading suburbs and congested tenements. And this new situation was fraught with economic and moral perils. The older conditions of Scottish life had afforded many safeguards against utter breakdown, whether moral or material. In the country parish, with its farmers, cottars, and trades-folk, people were supported in decent and honourable living by the public opinion of the community, the leaven of the Church, and probably the honourable tradition of their family, while in the day of calamity distress evoked a good response of neighbourly helpfulness and of Christian charity. In the new conditions it was easier both to succeed brilliantly and to fail disastrously; but whether men succeeded or went to the wall, almost all suffered some damage in the ordeal.

I.

THE SPIRITUAL DAMAGE OF THE NEW ORDER.

Even the successful did not come off scathless— those who, endowed with ability and enterprise, and getting hold of some stock of capital, became the captains of industry or commerce, and amassed their fortunes.   In the haste to grow rich, a severe strain was often put on their loyalty to the Scottish tradition of integrity.   The organisation of industry on the large scale to some extent substituted what Carlyle called the mere " cash-nexus " for the old friendly relations between the employer and the employed. Nor was their success invariably a blessing to their posterity.   It was not uncommon for the family of the prosperous manufacturer or merchant to become useless, if not in the second, at least in the third, generation, through neglect of the Biblical maxim that it is good for a man to bear the yoke in his youth.

2. The wage-earning class benefited largely by the new conditions and on the whole came well through the moral probation.   They commanded a much higher price for their labour, while the cost of the necessaries and the comforts of life was kept down by the inflow of the products of other lands.   Their days were spent in toil which, though often burdensome, and still more monotonous, was at least a discipline to themselves, and a service to mankind.   They pre-served in large measure many of the sterling qualities of the Scottish race—industry, independence, mental acquisitiveness, domestic purity, and public and patriotic spirit.   They usually gave their children the best education in their power.   They also clung on the whole to the faith of their fathers, as seen

in the existence of working-class congregations which have a membership running into thousands. But neither did these escape unharmed. The wage-earner's lack of a direct interest in the profits of the business with which he is connected goes far to explain the extraordinary development of gambling, which supplies the pleasures of hazard and hope in a less legitimate and remunerative but more rapid and sensational form. For the monotony not a few claimed compensation on one afternoon of the week, and perhaps a few days at the beginning of the year, by giving themselves a "moral holiday." They also tended to regard themselves—the working-classes proper—as a kind of nation within the nation, and questions of hours and wages gave to their minds a materialistic bent which contrasts a little painfully with the popular idealism of the bygone generations.

3. These were the strong, and what of the weak, the deficient in intelligence, or in energy, or in both? There was a large demand for their unskilled labour; and they gathered in great numbers in the manu-facturing towns, hung about the docks, took a hand in the making of railways and the building of houses, or lounged in the cities on the outlook for casual employment. Their position was one of great in-security owing to the progress of labour-saving inventions, the fluctuations of trade, and the revolution of the seasons. They were in frequent danger of finding themselves out of work, and were frequently face to face with the elementary problem of where

the next meal was to be found. Among them drunkenness found its ready victims. Unintelligent and weak of purpose, they had little hope and joy in life, and at the same time they made the fatal discovery of the very real consolations of strong drink. In the riot of an evening hour, they could feel the pleasure of living intensely—could forget the past, transfigure the present, and defy the future. And so with many the habit was formed which dragged them down to still lower depths of physical and moral debility.

4. And the weakness and the iniquity of bad parents were visited on their children. In the families of this class the infant mortality has hitherto been very great. In spite of miserable conditions of nurture and housing, a surprising number grow up to youth and manhood, but, left as they are without proper discipline and control, many are found to be incapable of sustained and useful work. What the situation would have been but for the beneficent work of the school, which for at least eight important years takes the chief command of their lives, may be left to the imagination. But the school is heavily handicapped in its moralising task. Blunted and coarsened as their feelings must be by early familiarity with the worst side of human nature, they are too often caught, before they are well aware of human responsibility, in the meshes of vice and even of crime.

5. For the women of Scotland the new conditions brought many changes, and not altogether for the

better. Whether the wives and daughters of the successful men were better women in the sunshine of fortune is a question which is open to debate. There has been no such deterioration as the prophets pictured in Samaria and Jerusalem, but the old sense of duty was considerably modified by the assertion of the right to pleasure, and the old simplicity by what the Apostle called the lust of the eye and the pride of life. To the women of the working-classes the new order of things, with its large demand on the economic service of women, was certainly not an unmixed blessing. The occupation of the factory girl is a poor preparation for married life, and when a married woman, as so often happens in our cities, combines the work of a breadwinner with that of a housekeeper, the result is often disastrous to the well-being both of herself and of her family. There was also a crop of still worse evils. It seems to be established that, even before the war, there was a serious increase of drinking among women. And the sins of the flesh are closely related, and are kind to their relations.

II.

THE PAST CONTRIBUTION OF THE CHURCH.

The evils which have followed as an attendant shadow upon our national prosperity have, of course, been observed and grappled with by a confederacy of agencies, political and religious, public and private.

And the Scottish Church has not been without a programme and a policy. From the Reformation downwards, it was recognised that the Church had a fourfold duty—to preach the gospel for the salvation of souls, to carry on a pastoral ministry for the improvement of families and individuals, to relieve the distress of the sick and the poor, and to see that the children were educated. With the great increase and shifting of the population of Scotland, the machinery of the Church proved inadequate for carrying out its programme. Its powers were even overtaxed to fulfil its primary function of spiritual ministry. Still more conspicuously was it unable to live up to the other parts of its tradition. The old theory was that every family in a given area should be reached by the inspiring and correcting influences of the Church, but the new communities were so large that many were unknown to the minister and his coadjutors. Whereas in the older time the Church made itself responsible for the relief of the poor, in the new conditions many congregations found themselves unable even to support the poor of their own households, and, in spite of the impassioned appeals of Chalmers, the notion of the Church undertaking to deal with the whole mass of national destitution was abandoned as Utopian. Similarly, it gave way to the State as the national educator. It seemed, in short, as if the Church had failed in respect of about three-fourths of its original proposals.

But this view would be superficial. If the Church retired from parts of the field it was because it had inspired and taught a more wealthy successor. The nation as such had imbibed so much of the Christian spirit as to make it in a real sense, and in ever-increasing measure, a philanthropist and an educationist. Since the middle of last century in particular, there has been a growing recognition that it is the business of the State to take measures to ensure that we shall bear one another's burdens. The conscience of Parliament has been steadily quickened, and the same is even more true of local corporations. All the signs go to show that more and greater things will be attempted, by means of the collective wisdom, wealth, and power, for the amelioration of social conditions, and for the restraint both of destructive vices and of the more painful forms of social injustice.

III.

THE SURVIVING TASK OF THE CHURCH.

What, then, is the special function of the Church in this field? It might seem as if, in the general progress of society, the Church is destined to be confined to the purely spiritual side of its original programme. And as a fact, if it should concentrate exclusively upon its spiritual work and concentrate effectually, it would continue to make an extremely important contribution, even of the social kind, to the well-being of society. If it be successful in preaching its spiritual gospel, it is successful in doing a great deal more. To persuade men to embrace a religion which engenders faith in a' holy and a loving God, which fills the heart with devotion to Christ, which gives a comforting and inspiring outlook upon life and destiny, which makes diligence and integrity a matter of principle, and which constrains to purity and moves to brotherly kindness —all this makes up a contribution of social service of which it is hardly possible to overestimate the value. When we consider that the Church possesses the only message which is known radically to transform the character of debased men and women, and on the other hand, that, of those who labour in the political or municipal spheres to brighten and purify the life of our people, very · many owe much of their best inspiration to their training by the' Church, we may be disposed to think that nothing else which the Church could do would be half so important as that it should be able to preach a renewing gospel in faith and with power, and to act as the nursery of Christian character.

In the second place, it is only just to recognise the very great ethical value of the social unit which we call a Christian congregation. In many ways the congregation is a very remarkable social institution. We should realise this vividly were it not that we are so prone to undervalue that which already exists, and to form extravagant expectations in regard to other schemes which have not yet been fully tested. From the social point of view, a congregation is a very remarkable creation, if only from the fact that it unites persons of every class and grade of culture, as well as of every period of life, in a society which is based on the principle of human brotherhood. Especially is this realised in the Holy Communion, where persons the most diverse meet at a common table on the footing of brothers and sisters holding a common faith and hope, and the menial office of serving tables is discharged by men who are deemed most worthy of honour by the society. From the numerous and ever-multiplying congregational agencies, Sunday schools, Bible classes, and guilds, which labour to form the principles and to mould the character of the young, there are very large if untabulated results of a moral and social kind — not to speak of the very important reflex influence of these labours in developing the human sympathies and the social conscience of the labourers. Further, we may be gratified by the fact that social workers have been recommending, as if it were a new discovery, a kind of machinery which the Church has long believed in, and which it has actually created and set in motion. In the cities we commonly divide a parish into districts, and attach to each an elder and one or more visitors, and our ideal is that they, as well as the minister, should come into personal contact with the people in their homes, and this is precisely the kind of organisation which according to the newer wisdom of the Charity Organisation Society is required to make a real and lasting impression on struggling persons and families. It is quite true that our general practice falls far short of our theory, and that many of us, ministers as well as elders, have hardly even appreciated the theory. But if the system were generally worked as it is worked at its best, the congregation would take its place among our institutions, not merely as a home of worship and a centre for the religious and moral training of the young, but as an institution of an absolutely indispensable kind for coming into effective and minute touch with the social conditions that are the nursery of so much distress and sin.

In addition to the familiar agencies of the congregation a more direct contribution has recently been made, under the name of social work, to the social mission of the Church of Scotland. Experience has shown that there is a large class of people who are not influenced by preaching, because they do not go to hear it, or by sympathetic visitation, because the chains of evil habit or the influence of a bad environment have become overpowering. In many cases the only reasonable hope of amendment lies in removing the individual to new surroundings, in which he will be sheltered from temptation, disciplined to work and self-control, and braced up to make a new start. The Church of Scotland, following the pioneer-work of the Salvation Army, has established lodging-houses, labour homes, and labour colonies in various parts of town and country. In the development of this social work narrowly so called, the Church of Scotland, even with the help of other Churches, is far from covering the whole ground in Scotland. If the needs of the case are to be adequately met, it will only be on the basis of a division of labour in which public bodies find the material support for the institutions, while the Church will mainly provide the workers without whom any schemes of the kind, at least as regards the highest results, must prove ineffective. But at the present juncture there are two good reasons why the Church should throw itself heartily into this work. One is that it is for her to convince the State by object-lessons that such rescue-work is well worth doing, and that even from the civic point of view it would be wise to support by adequate means a scheme which preserves and recovers valuable human material. The second reason is that even if the Church is unable to do all that is necessary, that is no justification for doing nothing at all. No work is more in the spirit of Him who was called the friend of publicans and sinners, as none is more hopeful when prosecuted by methods which reflect the combined care of our Lord's ministry for the souls and the bodies of men.

IV.

STRENGTHENING THINGS THAT REMAIN.

Although we may believe that it was inevitable and also desirable that the State should take over many of the functions which formerly entered into the social mission of the Church—notably in the matter of the care of the sick and the poor, and the education of the young—it is natural that those who love the Church should feel some misgiving at the process of denudation, which threatens to leave it with little direct interest in the programme of the works of mercy that was commended both in the preaching and in the life of its Founder, and was taken over as a precious charge by the Church of former days. Very natural, therefore, and proper is the desire to strengthen the things that remain, in so far as these are connected with her vocation, or are not otherwise adequately dealt with. Two duties may be mentioned, one of which has been brought into prominence, the other into existence, by the experiences and the consequences of the great war.

1. A call has come to the Christian Church for heart-searching as to whether it has fulfilled its duty as the instructor of the social conscience of the community. I have spoken with all the deep respect which I feel for the work of the Church in the conversion and the sanctification of souls, but in the light of experience we must say that modern Evan-

gelicalism was mistaken when it supposed that by the preaching of the gospel of individual salvation it would destroy the roots of every social evil. For one thing, there were comparatively few who underwent a definite conversion; and for another, the exhortations to sanctification were too general. During the bygone century it may be doubted if the ornaments of the Christian pulpit did as much as lay preachers like Ruskin and Carlyle to quicken the social conscience, and to commend lofty ideals in the various departments of secular life and labour. It is our conviction that Christ—that the moral law at its highest demand of justice and brotherhood—should rule in all spheres; and the Church ought to be able to work this out in more definite and concrete shape than it has been in the habit of doing in recent generations. It seems desirable that the Church should make clearer to its own mind, and to other minds, what is its ideal of a national life pervaded by justice and brotherhood, and what is its conception of the things that ought to be done by public and private action so as to bring us nearer the ideal. This will bring it at some points into the political field, and it is no doubt desirable that it should keep out of politics; but when politics concern themselves with moral questions—as has been and will be increasingly the case—it is difficult to see how the Church can say that it has no opinion on the subject, and no guidance to offer.

2. A special philanthropic duty has emerged as a

13

result of the war. The Scottish Church in all its branches has declared, not only with practical unanimity, but with characteristic strength of conviction, that the cause is just, and that the course taken by our country can be amply vindicated in the name of God, and in accordance with any intelligent application of the principles of Christ. Its members and adherents have been in hearty accord with the message of the pulpit. Its congregations have compiled impressive Rolls of Honour. They have vied with one another in the support of war charities, and in the dispatch of gifts to the men on war-service. But the question may well be raised whether our Church has adequately realised the claims upon its philanthropic ministry of those members who have been involved in the calamities of the war. It may be recommended, at least to every large congregation, to appoint a special committee charged with the interests of those connected with the congregation who are among the victims of the war. The first task would be to compile a register carefully setting out the particulars as to how any individuals or families have been affected on the economic side as the result of the casualties. Among them will be the soldier disabled by wounds or broken down by sickness, the mother bereaved of a son on whom she was dependent, the widow and the fatherless children. The committee would next ascertain exactly what provision was being made by public pensions, and by the numerous voluntary societies, to relieve the consequent distress. But the chief responsibility would be to determine whether, after taking account of the many helping agencies, there was not in many cases an important supplementary duty for the institution which claims the character of a Christian family. General schemes, however wise and liberal, do not fit all particular cases, and many cases would be found in which the congregation would feel the need of its own special fund, from which to give additional help to the bereaved, or to enable the disabled to make a better start in a new calling. In other cases the great requirement would be not money, but information, sympathy, and counsel. Above all, it may well be felt that the case of the fatherless children makes an irresistible appeal to the heart of a congregation that is worthy of the Christian name. Some families should be in a general sense adopted by the congregation. Many a childless couple, and many a good-hearted spinster, might well adopt a child in literal fashion out of an orphaned family. In any case a systematic and sustained effort should be made through the minister and the committee to supervise the education and the upbringing of the fatherless children, and to ensure as far as possible that the boys and girls will not find that, as a consequence of the father's sacrifice, their own lives have been ruined or marred. As some congregations are rich and some poor, the development of such a scheme as has been indicated would naturally lead to the linking together of such congregations in pairs or groups. In a Presbyterian Church, the Presbytery would naturally have a committee which would superintend, stimulate, and organise the work within its own area. Naturally also the General Assembly would take cognisance of the scheme, and probably appoint a special Committee of Assembly to guide and control the whole movement. For such a service from the Church there is a distinct place among the abounding philanthropic efforts of modern society, and also — though that is of lesser moment — it would help to dispel the idea, which some rather industriously disseminate, that the Church is too much like the priest and the Levite who passed the stricken man on the other side, and too little like the Samaritan who bound up his wounds, pouring in oil and wine.   Amen.

XIV

THE CONSECRATION OF OUR GOODS.

"David would not drink of it, but poured it out to the Lord."—1 CHRONICLES xi. 18.

ISRAEL was at war with the Philistines, and the hostile armies were facing one another in the uplands to the south of Jerusalem. The Philistines had seized Bethlehem; and as David, who commanded his army in person, gazed from his stronghold upon the camp of the invader, his soul was stirred within him. The men of his bodyguard caught the words— "Oh, that one would give me drink of the water of the well of Bethlehem, that is at the gate." It may have been a cry of home-sickness. His meaning may have been—"Would to God that I had never entered on, that I were free of, this life of bloodshed, and intrigue, and royal cares, and that I passed my days, like my father Jesse, among the sheep-cotes." It may be that he was filled with wrath at the insult offered to him by the Philistines in violating the soil of his beloved Bethlehem, and that he was forming a plan of attacking in force and regaining possession of the hallowed spot. The mighty men who stood by took his words literally, and supposed that, being thirsty, he craved a drink from the old well whose water he remembered from boyhood as the best in the world. "And the three broke through the host of the Philistines, and drew water out of the well of Bethlehem, that was by the gate, and took it, and brought it to David." But the king would not drink it. "Shall I drink," he said, "the blood of those men that have put their lives in jeopardy?" He felt that it was too sacred for his private use, and he poured it out on the ground before the Lord. The modern reader may think it was an ungracious act, but this is only because we have become unfamiliar with many ancient ideas and practices. It would be thought, not a slight, but an honour, by those to whom the libation or drink-offering was a well-known religious rite. When a distinguished man in our day receives a valuable presentation it is not thought that he makes light of it if he proposes that, instead of keeping it as his own property, he should make it over to the community for a public purpose; and no more would the mighty men feel slighted when David, instead of drinking the water, devoted it to a religious use, and poured it out as a drink-offering before the Lord.

Many ingenious morals have been drawn by preachers from the story of King David and the well of Bethlehem. But to-day we have no need to seek for fanciful parallels and far-fetched lessons. Our people feels, or ought to feel, as David felt when the mighty men placed their hard-won gift before him.

For our sakes a multitude of mighty men are at grips with the Philistines, and are seeking to break through the host with jeopardy of their lives. And it is not a mere drink from the well of Bethlehem, but Bethlehem itself and all it stands for, which is ours to have and to hold because of the valour and the self-sacrificing devotion of our mighty men. "The water," said the King, "is the blood of man"; and with equal truth we can at least say that there is a blood-mark on our possessions. And for us, as for David, the question arises as to how we are to use the things which have been secured to us at the jeopardy and the cost of men's lives. Are we to look on them in the old way as our own, with which we may do as we will? Or are we to look on them as hallowed, and to seek in a modern but still a very real sense to pour them out to the Lord?

I.

THE BLOOD-BOUGHT WEALTH.

The nearest parallel to the case of David is the position of those who have been enriched, or who at least find themselves much better off, as the result of the economic upheaval of the war. It was to be expected that, in the event of our country being involved in a great European conflict, there would be witnessed the arrest of industry and the stagnation of commerce; that on every hand there would be the crash of bankruptcy and ruin; that the poor would be plunged into

extreme destitution, and that there might even be out-
breaks of civil disorder due to popular agonies of want
and despair.   And no doubt many have suffered
grievously, and have been sorely taxed to make ends
meet when confronted with ever-growing charges upon
fixed or even diminishing incomes; while as certainly
very heavy penalties will have to be paid in the
future by the nation as a whole for an unparalleled
expenditure which, instead of reproducing and aug-
menting the wealth of the country, is rapidly using it
up in a work of destruction.   But in the meantime
our country has in general had the appearance of
enjoying an era of unwonted prosperity.   Fortunes
have been made in shipping, mining, manufacturing,
and other vital industries; the agricultural classes
have been reaping a golden harvest; groups of
mechanics engaged on munitions of war have had
their wages doubled or trebled; a multitude of women
who seemed to be without a vocation have had their
services requisitioned in the office, the shop, the
factory, and the transport-service; wives of soldiers
who earned a precarious subsistence as unskilled and
casual labourers are in the enjoyment of a steady and
fairly liberal income; while in numberless instances
the earnings of families, even where the individual
wage has not increased, have reached a far higher
total than in ordinary times.   If the nation as a
whole, viewed merely in relation to its wealth, is like
nothing so much as a prodigal scattering a great inheritance to the winds, there are many individuals,

and even whole classes, who remind us of the friends and hangers-on of the prodigal, who busily make hay while the sun shines, and collect a handsome private profit and provision out of his ruthless extravagance.

But it is not only those that have made profit out of the war who are debtors to our valiant defenders. Those whose circumstances are much the same as before, and those who have become poorer, may well ponder the misfortunes from which they have been preserved by the protecting shield which has been thrown around them. Not to dwell on the higher things which have been imperilled—the existence of our Empire, the mission of our race, and our cherished liberties—it is evident that our material possessions have been conserved to us, and, as it were, repurchased for us, by the privations, sufferings, and deaths of those who undertook to defend us. The ordinary mind has scarcely realised the tremendous difference which it makes when a country, instead of being a theatre of war like Belgium and Northern France, abides in general peace and security like our homeland, and sends its armies to fight their battles on foreign soil. We may murmur at the increased cost of living, but our imagination ought rather to be picturing to us the distress which would overtake the population of our over-crowded island if our Fleet lost command of the ocean, and if even for three months we were deprived of the supplies of food from the lands beyond the seas. Some of us writhe under the burden of increasing taxation, forgetting that, if it were in the power of

Germany to dictate terms, not only would the British
Empire be plundered on a scale on which no State was
ever looted since the dawn of history, but for almost
every family the future would hold a predestined
struggle with penury and hardship.   It is, in short,
hardly an exaggeration to say that in this war Britain
has risked everything except its soul, and that the
reason why our possessions are still ours and will, we
believe, continue to be ours, is that there were men
enough who thought that we and our belongings were
worth fighting for and worth dying for.

II.

THE SACRED OBLIGATION.

In the next place it must be felt to be appropriate
that those whose wealth has been won or preserved at
the cost of men's blood should be impelled to devote
it to a high and sacred use.   As David said that the
water from the well of Bethlehem was the blood of
his brave men, which he could not drink to quench
his thirst, so it may well be thought that it is unseemly
and even odious to claim what the war has given us
for the selfish uses which passed without criticism in
ordinary times.   To the judgment of many of us it
seems inconceivable that, if the organisation of the
war could have been carried out with leisure and
deliberation, it would have been tolerated that some
men who were already wealthy should wring additional

fortunes out of the agony of their country, and that large groups of skilled labourers should be paid exorbitant wages while their former comrades who went into the death-zone were remunerated with a comparative pittance. In the case of those of us who have been made neither richer nor poorer it may also be thought to be an example of bad management, if not of inequitable dealing, that the Government leaves us to the undisturbed enjoyment of three-fourths of our incomes, comforts, and luxuries, while it has laid its hands upon the person and the services of every man, not otherwise of vital use to the State, who is capable of bearing arms against the enemy. But whatever may be thought of such anomalies, it is at least evident that those who have been thus favoured have no moral right to use their possessions as the means for the gratification of merely private inclinations and ambitions. For once in a way in the history of the modern world the principle has to be recognised that wealth is held on the terms of a stewardship, and that possessions are of the nature of a trust. To-day it is not a negligible counsel of perfection, but the plain common-sense view, that individual rights ought, as the rule, to be in abeyance, and that the only permissible question is how such means and such services as are at our command can be most wisely placed at the disposal of our country, and most effectively utilised in the maintenance of our country's cause. In view of the needs of our Empire in this crisis, as well as of the price at which they have been insured, our possessions have for the time acquired a character of sanctity; and we are impelled to ask, What is the modern fashion in which we are to follow the example of David, who poured out before the Lord the consecrated water from the well of Bethlehem?

The present-day parallel is that out of our means we should help the country to the utmost of our power in what we believe to be a sacred cause. That there is need of all the help which every citizen can give, if the war is to end as we desire it to end, is absolutely certain. Our country is enormously wealthy, and it has so far triumphantly stood a terrific financial strain, but its ready resources are not inexhaustible. Should the war be prolonged, as it may well be prolonged, to the end of 1917 or even longer, it is not impossible that—unless the nation awakens to the need of economy in a way of which there is at present little sign, or unless other measures are taken to cope with the financial situation—we might be driven to conclude a premature and disastrous peace. The second important consideration is that while the need of the State is clamant and imperious, a benevolent Government has followed its custom of following after the things which make for popularity, and has smoothed to the utmost the path of duty. It has not forgotten that the impulses of our human nature are an extraordinary compound of self-interest and self-sacrifice, and it has arranged that our self-denial shall be made as attractive and remunerative as possible. Those who are bearing the brunt of the armed struggle have, of course, to show self-sacrifice enough of the old kind, with new elements of danger, terror, and suffering thrown in ; but we who abide in the security and comfort of the mother-country are treated with the consideration which is always expected when monetary interests are in question, and we have the opportunity not only of discharging a sacred duty, but of obtaining on our loans the highest rate of interest which was ever offered by the British Treasury.

III.

WAYS OF DISCHARGING THE DUTY.

There are three chief ways in which response may be made to the appeal of our country for financial help in the present crisis.

1. The first and the most obvious, but not the all-sufficient method—is that those who are in possession of wealth which they had previously amassed or in-herited should proceed to lend it to the State. As a fact, a large proportion of the colossal loans which have been raised by the Government, amounting to over £2,000,000,000, have been obtained from accumulated wealth, such as the deposits lodged with the banks, and by selling home and foreign securities. But the point which it is specially important to emphasise is that an immense amount of wealth which in ordinary times can be converted into the form of money or credits cannot be got hold of for

the purposes of the war.   In normal circumstances a
rich man, whose riches was represented by a landed
estate, houses, Consols, or railway shares, could at
longer or shorter notice get it realised in terms of
money, and could devote the proceeds to some new
and special purpose, but under present conditions this
is sometimes impossible or may be objectionable.   In
many instances the wealth simply cannot be realised.
At the same time every one ought to realise all that
can be got for this purpose without manifest injustice
to himself or to others.

2. The second method is to increase production by
adding to the national stock of wealth which is being
brought into existence in the course of the war.   As
a fact a vast number of people who were previously
unproductive have been impressed into the service of
society, and many others have more than doubled
their social usefulness.   It entailed a very serious
dislocation of the social fabric when millions of men
were diverted from industry, commerce, and agricul-
ture for enlistment in the fighting forces and the
auxiliary services, and it is astonishing that there
should have been forthcoming a reserve of labour-
power which has not only averted a breakdown, but
has made it possible largely to meet the demands of
trade, and to supply us with our customary comforts
and conveniences.

Thousands of men have discovered that they had a
stock of energy and skill which was only waiting to be
called upon ; and it is computed that nearly a million

women have entered upon fields of labour which yield unexpected pleasure and profit to themselves as well as invaluable service to the State. For groups of schoolboys a most rational form of holiday has been devised by sending them to labour in a timber-camp or in the ingathering of the harvest. Misgivings and prejudices which in other days condemned many persons to a wholly or partially useless existence—as that it was beneath their dignity to work, or took the bread out of other people's mouths —have been temporarily swept away; and it is generally realised that every one who can find suitable work is a benefactor of the country, and that if only it be useful, there need be no further question as to whether it be consistent with one's station. The value of genuinely productive work which yields food or other necessaries, it may be added, is threefold—it adds to the store available for the supply of national wants, it helps to keep down the price demanded for the commodity from the needy, and it gives the producer more command of the money for which the Chancellor of the Exchequer is appealing.

3. The third method of procuring the means of a response to the national appeal is by way of the retrenchment of expenditure. The subject has its difficulties—especially when we undertake to criticise our neighbour's expenditure instead of our own, but one or two guiding principles may be somewhat confidently laid down. The general principle is that we ought to be willing to give up anything or everything

in our mode of life which is not required for health and efficiency. All expenditure, which is of the nature of luxury, or which is due merely to the desire of pleasure and excitement, or the love of display, or to the custom of our class and station, is to be subjected to the most suspicious and rigorous criticism. In the second place, we are warned by economists that we should be specially frugal in the purchase of goods which must eventually be paid for by remitting money to foreign countries. A third and qualifying principle is that some consideration must be shown by society for those whom it taught to depend for a livelihood on ministering to its whims and supplying it with its luxuries and its pleasures.

To some extent the bearing of these principles is obvious. It cannot be seriously maintained that it is necessary to the health and the efficiency of our people that it should spend half a million a day on alcoholic liquor. That sum amounts to about one-twelfth of the national income; it must be the same on the average for the individual; and it is difficult to conceive a man drawing out a budget in these times, and deliberately setting apart one-twelfth of his income to the purchase of wine, beer, and spirits. For want of scientific knowledge the money spent on food is to a large extent misspent. If it be true, as has been stated, that £300,000,000 is spent annually by women on dress, it should be possible under this head to effect a national gain that would rival the saving on the drink bill. There is also a large amount of expenditure in the upkeep of great establishments which, dubious enough at any time, has become indefensible. But, clear as the general principles are, their application is made difficult by the fact that our lives are largely ruled by custom. Among the poorer classes custom has often the power of a tyranny, and among the better-off classes its claims have been hardly less imperious. The wealthier classes had adopted a mode of living in which luxury and display were deemed entirely justifiable; and it is not an easy matter for an individual or a family to disentangle themselves from the conventional ways, nor can it always be done with immediate advantage. One possession which may challenge criticism in the light of our principles, and also illustrates the difficulty, is the dwelling-house. Some of us find ourselves in the occupation of houses which are not proportioned to our needs, but were perhaps selected because of the pleasure we feel in spacious rooms, or our sense of the rights and requirements of our position; and it may be that, while we know that the house is with us the key to the economic situation, a change cannot be carried out in the circumstances of the time without grievous loss to the individual, and with the assured certainty of social benefit. At the same time there must be some in a great city who see their way to solve the problem of the large house in a way that will greatly increase their power of social service. If it is

14

possible to make over a house which one does not fully utilise for some public purpose, or to let it to another occupant who would take full advantage of its social utilities, there does not seem any good reason why even a rich man or woman should not go into a modest flat for the period of the war, and make trial of existence under the simpler conditions in which countless human beings after all live useful and contented lives. Another experiment which could be recommended from the point of view of the stress of the times, were it not almost certain to be shattered on British individualism, would be to use the large house as the home of two or more families and to unite them by the bond of a co-operative housekeeping. Apart from this difficult central problem, there are many details of luxury and display in the arrangements of the rich, and to some extent of the poor, which will not stand examination in the light of the needs of the time. But it must be left to individuals to think out the bearing of the principles upon the concrete details of their daily lives, and to consider how their outgoings may be so reduced as to bring them within the circle, if they are not already in it, of those who are making sacrifices that are adequate to their country's need.

The call for saving is so imperative that it will have to be effected in one way if not in another. The alternative is to compel us to save by taxing us to the utmost limit, and taking a compulsory loan out of the remainder of our income; and it is quite possible that, if the war be prolonged, our rulers will be driven to adopt such methods. It is not improbable that, just as the appeal for men finally issued in conscription, so the appeal for money will finally issue in compulsory borrowing. And though some of us may think that the compulsory measures would be more effective, we ought to strain every nerve to ensure the success of the voluntary scheme. After all, it is better for us that we should do our duty willingly and cheerfully than that we should be driven to do it. It may be necessary that the burden of privation should be laid upon us, but it is better for character and life that we should take up the cross of self-denial and so follow our Master. Amen.

XV

THE BIBLE-PICTURE OF WOMAN.

"And the Lord God said, It is not good that the man should be alone; I will make him an help meet for him."—GENESIS ii. 18.

ONE of the most interesting chapters in the history of the human race is the story of the rise and progress of woman. We can distinguish four stages of an ascending scale, although it need not be supposed that these have followed in chronological order in every progressive country. The lowest stage is that in which woman was treated as a beast of burden. This is her lot amongst savage peoples, and also amongst those in which there is a large survival of the conditions of the lower culture. It is sufficiently illustrated by the report of a traveller that a tribe of American Indians supposed that the oxen which they yoked to their carts were the wives of the white settlers. A second, and somewhat higher stage, is represented by the view, which is especially distinctive of the Oriental civilisations, that woman has the character of a toy or plaything, and exists merely for the pleasure of the man. A third conception, met with in the Middle Ages, assigned to her the rank of goddess.   Faith in womanhood was a cardinal article of the creed of the Age of Chivalry.

> "Angels are painted fair to look like you;
> There's in you all that we believe of Heaven,
> Amazing brightness, purity, and truth,
> Eternal joy and everlasting love."

This high estimate, however, did not always or necessarily involve corresponding practical reforms in the arrangements of everyday life. The fourth and highest stage is that in which the woman is accorded substantial equality with the man, and is treated as his coadjutor and friend.

The causes which have led to the gradual improvement in the position of woman are many, and the elevating influences have come from various quarters. Something has to be attributed to the fact that the man has a conscience, and that moral forces are permanently at work in human society—of which there is a relevant and striking illustration in the fact that, without agitation or compulsion from the feminine side, civilised humanity finally decided to establish the institution of monogamous marriage. It has been said that woman's position was permanently raised by the provision of the Roman Law which gave her the right to hold and control property. The influence of the modern poets has on the whole been on her side—and not least the influence of the greatest. Broadly speaking, Ruskin's contention is true that Shakespeare has no heroes, only heroines. "The catastrophe of every play," he says, "is caused always by the fault or folly of a man; the redemption, if there be any, is by the wisdom of a woman, and failing that there is none." And, finally, she owes an immeasurable debt to the Christian religion, which taught that man is made in the image of God and shares his dignity with the woman, and which laid down the principle that in Christ Jesus there is neither male nor female—that the equality of the sexes is perfect and absolute in the purely spiritual sphere. St. Paul, indeed, guarded against the idea that the equality extends to all spheres, and spoke of a natural subordination and duty of obedience; but this has a justification in the world's division of labour, and especially in the fact that provision has to be made in all human affairs for a final court of appeal.

The Bible as a whole shows great reverence for woman. One of the features of the Bible which stamps it as the Word of God is that it knows so fully what is in man, and, it may be added, that it has so deep an insight into what is characteristic of woman. In general, it may be said that in the Bible woman is far more highly esteemed, and fills a much more important place, than was usual in the ancient world. Though it is a collection of ancient literature, some of it very old, and though it has come to us from Asia, the Bible is in this respect the precursor of the modern and western view of woman. It does not indeed make of her an idol, as has been done by poets and romancers with their " mystical veneration for the feminine elements of humanity." It frankly gives examples of characteristic failings and dangers. But it also gives striking instances of the nobler qualities which, it conceives, make up the normal outfit of the better samples of womanhood. It is impossible to do more than sketch slightly the Bible-picture of woman, but we may at least select some of the chief things which have the character of warnings or appreciations.

I.

WARNINGS.

Beginning with the warnings, we find that the opening chapters of the Bible contain an interesting psychological study, which also carries with it a serious admonition. When sin entered into the world, it is said that the Tempter selected the woman for his assault, insiduously overcame her scruples, and by using her as his tool prevailed upon the man also to break a positive commandment of God. How far the story of the first temptation, and of the Fall, is to be received as literal history, is a question on which theologians have differed since the second century; but it is at least agreed that the narrative contains a great deal of truth about the workings of human nature, and the stages of an experience which begins with a temptation, and ends in sin, punishment, and remorse. The woman is tempted to eat of the tree of the knowledge of good and evil. It has been thought inappropriate that the woman should be tempted by offering her something good to eat. Temptation, it is thought, comes to the man rather than the woman in the pleasures of the table, but the point rather is that she is so constituted that she feels a strong impulse to yield for the mere reason that the thing is forbidden. She is given to understand that if she eats of the tree there will be opened up to her a world of knowledge of which she is ignorant, and she finds the prospect irresistible. The same point has been emphasised by folklore in the old story of Bluebeard and his wife. It explains the fate of many a daughter of Eve whose life has ended in a vulgar tragedy. It also produces the emaneipated woman, so familiar a figure in modern literature, who in many of the varieties is not so much shocking as irritating and unpleasant.

2. A second warning, given in two stories from the days of the patriarchs, is that woman is in danger of setting love above conscience. Abraham had two wives, Sarah and Hagar, each of whom bore him a son. Sarah was jealous of Ishmael, the son of the bondwoman, feared that he might divide the inheritance with her own son Isaac, and persuaded Abraham to send away the son along with the slave-wife, so that they might perish in the wilderness. In her turn Rebecca, the wife of Isaac, had two sons, Esau and Jacob. Jacob, who was the younger, was her favourite, and she taught him how to deceive the aged Isaac, so that he might rob the elder brother

of his father's blessing.   In both stories the point is the same: that a woman, inspired by a mother's love, was guilty in one case of injustice, in another even of vindictive cruelty.   The same idea has been expressed in various ways by modern writers.   It was said by Herbert Spencer that her sense of justice is less developed than that of the man.   From some works of fiction we gather that she does not feel an obligation to tell the truth, and to act uprightly, when honesty would run counter to the interests of those she loves.   This is the motive of one of the best known of Ibsen's plays, in which a woman cannot see that she has done any wrong when she procures by fraud the money that will save the life of her invalid husband, by sending him to recuperate for the winter on the Mediterranean.   When he finds out what she has done he is shocked at the crime, and she can only glory in her sacrifice.   On the other hand, one remembers that Sir Walter allowed nothing of this sophistry in Jeanie Deans.   The bias of the heart can be respected, but it is certain that while love is the fulfilling of the law, it is not an apology for breaking other moral laws.

3. A third warning which is written large in the annals of the Bible is that woman is capable of becoming terribly perverted—of doing things which are utterly contrary to the deepest womanly instincts, and even perhaps falling to lower depths of degradation than the man.   Modesty is a feminine grace, but the Old Testament mentions some scandalous exceptions—

notably Potiphar's wife. A woman is naturally sympathetic and kind-hearted, but there are women of the Bible who are more pitiless and bloodthirsty than the worst of the wicked men of their surroundings——Jezebel for example, who stirred up Ahab to put the prophets of Jehovah to the sword; Athaliah, who arose and slew all the seed royal of the house of Judah; and Herodias and her daughter, who, when Herod shrank from the crime, persisted in demanding the head of John the Baptist on a charger. Amos and Isaiah, when describing the sins of Israel and of Judah, declared that the worst. of all were the women of fashion, who seemed to have changed their nature into that which was against nature, and who even surpassed their lords in luxury and pride, in covetousness and inhumanity. But even in mentioning these examples it may be thought that the Bible pays a tribute to woman, for it is an old observation that, when the best things are corrupted, they are apt to become the very worst.

II.

APPRECIATIONS.

Turning to the other side of the picture, we have remarked generally that the position of woman in Bible times was one of unusual dignity and influence. Notable women appear alongside of the great figures of the Old Testament history, share in their councils and their labours, and are even the instruments by which weighty affairs are settled and great deliverances are effected. Sarah and Rebekah strike us as having stronger wills, if not also stronger minds, than Abraham and Isaac. Miriam was not wholly eclipsed even by Moses. Deborah seems to have been as resolute and vigorous in action as Barak, and also to have been more gifted in speech. To Esther the Jews of a later period attributed the escape of their people from the snares of a cruel enemy, and even from total destruction. And it was the same in humbler spheres. In the Book of Proverbs there is the picture of a good woman to whom her husband chiefly owes it that he is able to buy fields, and sits among the elders of the land. We shall touch on some of the higher qualities which are manifested by woman in the Bible narratives, and which go to explain the position of honour which was accorded her in the times which are illuminated by the sacred history.

1. It would appear, to begin with, that the Bible is pervaded by a deep impression of the wisdom of woman. It is she who often offers the prudent counsel in difficult situations. When David was once hard pressed by Saul, he was saved by the wits of his wife. Later, when he is plunged in gloom and indecision, it is a wise woman of Tekoa who weaves a tale that rouses him from his lethargy, and gives him a plan of action. There is a little maid of Samaria who, when they are discussing the desperate case of Naaman the leper, makes known how he may

hope to be cured of his leprosy. Esther, though her spirit and methods were not above reproach, was at least always mistress of the situation. The New Testament gives us fewer instances of clever initiative and contrivance. But, on the other hand, it was among the women that much of the insight was found in the period of the origins of the Christian society. The infant Christ was welcomed to the temple by Anna the prophetess as well as by Simeon, and there is no song of Joseph the carpenter to be sung along with the Magnificat of Mary. When the gospel was carried to Athens, and the wisdom of this world proved to be blindness, there were two who recognised the true light—Dionysius the Areopagite, and a woman named Damaris. It is clear that our Lord during His ministry sometimes turned to the believing women for the understanding and sympathy which He failed to get from the other disciples. Chiefly did He find this divine wisdom in Mary of Bethany.

2. A second distinctive womanly quality, if we may so infer from the many examples given in Scripture, is courage. When Pharaoh, King of Egypt, resolved to exterminate the Israelites by putting to death all the male children, the Egyptian nurses, we are told, were bold enough to defy him, and to save the children alive. Even the daughter of Pharaoh took one of the Hebrew infants into her house. Deborah sounded the trumpet which put courage into the heart of the Israelite host, and Jael, though we

may dislike her treatment of a trustful guest, had at least the courage to take a nail and a hammer and make an end of the dreaded scourge of her country. When Jesus was delivered into the hands of His enemies, and the disciples forsook Him and fled, the women of the company remained near, and followed Him to Calvary. When the persecutions broke out at a later time, women as well as men were haled to prison, and some of them doubtless went willingly, as in later ages, to a martyr's death. The general impression, in fact, which is left is that women not only have as much moral courage as men—at least when heart and conscience unite to bind them to a cause—but that they have also far more physical courage than it is usual to credit them with, and than they are accustomed to show in presence of minor dangers and petty issues.

3. The feminine quality which appears in the Bible as almost the most distinctive is that persistence of affection and purpose for which we have the names of loyalty, fidelity, or constancy. It has a famous illustration in the story of Ruth. A woman of Israel, called Naomi, went to sojourn in the land of Moab; her two sons married daughters of the land; the sons died, and the old woman returned to her native place. One of the daughters-in-law went back to Moab, but Ruth clave to her, saying, "Where thou goest, I will go, and where thou dwellest, I will dwell; thy people shall be my people, and thy God, my God." We may think this another example of a woman sacrific-

ing principle to personal affection; love, it would seem, should not dictate to her what God she was to serve; but since in this case the true religion went with constancy in love, she was for once justified in taking a characteristic line. And, not to multiply examples, loyalty is the common trait of the women who gathered in the following of Jesus. They followed Him from Galilee to Jerusalem; they remained beside the cross when the rest forsook Him. When Jesus was laid in the tomb, and all seemed at an end, they bethought them that one duty still remained, and they came to the sepulchre with the spices which they had prepared for the embalming of the body. No woman appears alongside of the traitor; nor does Paul make mention of any woman who, like Demas, forsook him, having loved this present world. A hundred years later Pliny, a Roman Governor, noted the quality in Christians of both sexes, pronounced it inflexible obstinacy, and was confirmed by what happened when he put two women to the torture.

The quality of loyalty is a markedly feminine grace. In the religious sphere it strongly disposes her to a conservatism which clings somewhat tenaciously to old beliefs, old ideals, and old customs. It is true that she has sometimes cast in her lot with those who welcomed the new or reformed the old. In the first age, as we have seen, there were ardent women among the first converts and the first pioneers of the gospel. At the Reformation it does not appear that women as a class stood by the old order, while not a few were prominent within the circle of the leading Reformers.   In these cases the new offered them something which seemed to them even more precious than the old associations, or the old was found to be in conflict with something which they prized even more than tradition or custom.   The women who followed Jesus had been touched in their hearts, and He also had given them woman's treasured possession of hope.   The women of the Reformation era were probably alienated from the Roman Church by the scandals of the clergy, and by the feeling that its system of prohibited degrees made marriage insecure.   On the whole, however, the woman has been the conservative factor in religious history, while the man has been more ready to seek for new light, to entertain fresh ideas, and to initiate practical changes.   And it is evident that both factors have been necessary to further the interests of true religion.   It was of vital importance that the human race should have a mind which was open to consider the new—else there would have been no planting of the Christian religion, and no triumph of the Protestant Reformation ; and this principle of religious movement and progress has on the whole been entrusted to the men.   It is of equal moment to the race that nothing of the spiritual patrimony, nothing especially of the Christian inheritance, which is of real value should be lost in transmission from one generation to another, and this task has been mainly committed, by reason of their essential fidelity, to the ministry of the women. Even in the Christian age, when the teaching office of the clergy, and religious instruction in schools, have attained such importance, the mother and the nurse have retained a vast influence in determining what is to be handed on to the new generation, and in making up for the children their abiding private store of religious beliefs and moral maxims, of sacred histories and spiritual songs. And in this work there has usually been seen the mark of pious veneration for the old. In our time the value of the co-operation of the ministries of change and conservation has been somewhat strikingly illustrated. The progress of theology has been almost exclusively due to the masculine mind, but on the other hand womanly conservatism has had a powerful restraining influence in preserving the world against the invasion of a no-gospel of mere doubts and denials.

4. The Bible confirms the impression that woman as woman has deeply religious instincts. It would be untrue to say that she did more than fill a secondary and subordinate place in the course of the progressive Revelation which is mirrored in the Scriptures. The Scriptures are largely concerned with creative and formative periods of religious history; and as originality of the first order has seldom been displayed by women in the other higher departments of the activities of the human spirit, such as the arts and philosophy, so was it to be

expected that in the great religious periods her function would on the whole be receptive and appreciative.   At the same time it is true that some of the creative personalities of the Old Testament even appear in a relation of somewhat close dependence upon women of their family and household.   Moses declared that the God whom he revealed to Israel was no new deity, but the God of their forefathers; and we seem to be left to gather that Moses owed his knowledge of the patriarchs and of their God to the mother who remained his nurse after she had given up her son to Pharaoh's daughter.   The next commanding figure after Moses is Samuel, and it is mentioned that his mother was a devout woman, and that she dedicated her son to the Lord from the womb.   The New Testament has striking instances of the same kind.   We are prepared for the advent of John the Baptist, the last of the prophets and the herald of the new dispensation, by an account of the faith and the hopes of Elisabeth his mother.   There are disappointingly few details in the Gospels about James the son of Zebedee and John his brother, but room is found for a picture of the woman in whose passion and devotion we can readily recognise the mother of the disciple whom Jesus loved.   We would fain know more of the woman who was honoured to be the mother of the Lord.   We at least know that in Mary there dwelt the perfected spirit of Old Testament piety, and we also have a glimpse of the guardian of the childhood of Jesus in the report of

15

the mother who kept the great events and promises of the infancy, and who pondered them in her heart. In the later ages of the Christian Church, also, there has usually been discernible, near the greater personalities, the influence of the hand and mind of a devout woman. The man whom the Church in all its branches has agreed to call supremely great is Augustine, and the two powers which—himself being witness—made him what he became were the grace of God and the prayers of Monica his mother.

If even in the creative periods of religion as represented by the Bible the influence of woman was considerable, it is natural that she has played a much more prominent part in those epochs of the Christian Church which have been, not golden ages, but only ages of silver, or of some baser metal. In times marked by spiritual inferiority or decadence her spiritual receptiveness and her fidelity to trust have accounted for a large part of such true religion as existed. Just as there are some nations which as a whole are more religious by natural endowment than others, so it seems to be established that for the female sex as a whole religion means more than it does for the male sex. There are two considerations which seem to explain why it is so. In the first place, a very distinctive feature of religious experience is the sense of dependence upon God—many have held that this is even the essence of religion. But the general conditions of the lot of woman are such as to foster in her a general sense of dependence

upon a higher power, since to a greater extent than
for the man her life is felt to be mapped out for her,
and to be moulded by forces which at the outset were
incalculable and unforeseen. And just as there is
more piety among those classes of men—as fisher-
men and to a lesser degree peasants—whose life-work
constantly brings home to them their dependence,
than there is among the tradesmen and artisans of the
cities, so is it natural that the sex which has most of
the same experience should have a deeper and a
more constant spirit of religion. In yet another way
does woman appear to have been specially made for
religion, and to have a special affinity with the
Christian religion. The essential thing in religion is
that it is an experience which consists in communion
between two persons—the human worshipper and
the living God. While morality is the keeping of a
law, religion is the friendship of the human with the
divine spirit : Christian experience, in its most characteristic and refined form, consists in the communion
of the believing soul with its risen and glorified Lord.
The spiritual constitution of woman, now, is such that
she is more interested in persons than in abstract
truths and ideals. Men can take a more independent
interest in ideas, policies, philosophies : women are
largely drawn to them in the measure in which they
are represented by or embodied in persons whom
they can revere and trust. The result is that, while
man's religion often resolves itself into a mere scheme
of religious doctrines, or obedience to a moral law,

while in some developments it loses hold even of the personality of God, the instincts of woman keep her mindful of the truth that the chief privilege of our existence is the possibility of the communion of the soul with the living God, and that our ideas of salvation and of duty are embodied in the Christ who, after enduring the Cross and despising the shame, has been exalted to the right hand of God.

Tertullian said of the soul that it has in a sense a natural endowment of Christianity, and the same may be said of womanhood. But the last word must be, that woman shares with the man, not only the image of God, but also the sinful inheritance, and that no flesh may glory in His presence. Amen.

XVI.

IN QUEST OF TRANQUILLITY.

"Oh that I had wings like a dove! for then would I fly away,
and be at rest."—Ps. lv. 6.

IF it should be announced at some great gathering
in a city hall that after the manner of the fairy
tales every one present was to be allowed to name a
wish, and that the request would be granted, the
counting of the votes would be extremely interesting.
There would be two main classes: those who asked
for themselves, and those who asked for others. Of
those who sought their own good some would doubtless ask for health; some for love to encircle and
bless their lives; some for fame and power; a few,
like Solomon, for wisdom; the majority, in all likeli-
hood, would ask for riches, or at least for a comfortable fortune. It would, however, still be a question
whether they were applying for what they most
deeply needed, and even whether there was not in
their mind the reservation that what they asked was
a means to a further end, and that this end was tranquillity of soul. Certain it is that the great question
which men have been putting everywhere and always

is how and where the soul is to enter into its rest.

Human nature is essentially restless. Many have been struck by the contrast in this respect between man and the lower animals. A child does not seem to enjoy existence quite as much as a frolicking lamb or puppy, and Walt Whitman spoke for at least some others when he looked with envy on the placid self-satisfied mood of a herd of cows. It would also appear that we Scottish people have even more than our share of the unquiet mind. The Providence which endowed our stock with many useful and respectable qualities set repose before us in the light of an achievement rather than of a gift. The probability is that tranquillity of mind is even less common than an observer might be disposed to think. There are a great many who obviously are unhappy; and when we add those who, though joyless at heart, are too proud to show it, or too well-bred not to keep up an apparent flow of spirits, we may be sure that there is a very widespread demand for the secret of peace. As a fact, the conditions of human life are such that man may seem to be predestined to unrest. Our natural desires are many and exorbitant, and only a few of them can be gratified as they propose, or even gratified at all. We have a conscience which makes us uncomfortable, and even torments us if we defy it; and our lives are full of habits or actions which amount to a defiance of conscience. Our affections are fixed on possessions, or on kindred and friends, that are hostages for our happiness, and we hold them all by a more or less precarious tie. We are travelling into an unknown future, in which it is certain that we shall be smitten, bruised, and impoverished by the forces of change and decay, and that in it there awaits us the inevitable event which, it may be with merciful suddenness, it may be after a period of weakness and agony, will carry us away from the light of the sun and from most of the things which have made for our happiness. These grim conditions, which are always with us, have been intensified of late: the rate of calamity has been accelerated, and its ravages have extended into every circle. And the wonder is, not that man is restless, but that he takes the situation, on the whole, so calmly. The explanation is that it is alleviated to a considerable degree by the power of habit. It is said that, in the neighbourhood of the trenches in France, old men and women may be seen cultivating the fields in indifference to the occasional shell that bursts around them, and that birds nestle even in the no-man's-land, and soar heavenward singing their carols as blithely as in the days of old. In like manner there are many who are able to forget the tragical setting of the world they live in, and to sing songs, not because they have mastered the situation, but because they have found it possible to ignore its darker side.

We pass on to the very practical question of the remedy. The subject is not one which has been overlooked. The work of the world goes on because the world has a working theory as to the secret of peace. Every great religion that has gained a footing among men has prescribed some treatment of the malady. The urgency of the need was observed by Him who knew what is in man, and much of Christ's teaching circled round rest and peace. Let us glance briefly at some of the other famous specifics, and then consider the provisions which are made for dealing with the evil in the Christian gospel.

I.

THE PRESCRIPTION OF THE NATURAL MAN.

To begin with, as I said, the world has its working theory as to the secret of rest. It is that, if we are miserable, it is because we have not enough of this world's goods, or that we have too much of its evils. If he made his fortune, one thinks, another, if he were famous, another, if he had power, and so on, he would then be within sight of the sovereign good. Others, especially as life advances, think that if only they could escape from their labours, and exchange the heavy and monotonous drudgery for sheltered leisure, they would find the pearl of price. And the philosophical observer has smiled at these hopes as illusions, and written essays and satires on the subject. They are, he admits, useful illusions. The world's work would not be so efficiently done were it not that it promises more satisfaction than will ever be got out of its results.   He also advises those who are looking to find peace later, and outside of their work, rather to look for it now and along with their work, and to make the most of the possible joys of the passing day.   But on the main issue it seems established that rest of soul is not guaranteed by success in the pursuit of the blessings of this world. One may gain all, and more than all, that he sought of the prizes of the world, and yet remain a miserable man.   He may be without them, and yet be at peace. No wise man will despise the natural blessings of life, but also no wise man will believe that of themselves they are a sufficient medicine for the deep-seated malady of the soul.

II.

THE REMEDY OF ASCETICISM.

At the opposite extreme from the workaday theory is a prescription which, fanatical and absurd as it seems to us, has played a great part in religious history.   The advice given is that man, instead of seeking peace in the acquisition of worldly goods, should seek it by renouncing and despising them.   It is a doctrine which has had a strong attraction for the people of India.   It was illustrated by the great renunciation of Buddha.   He was born and grew up in a court, he was the heir to a throne, he married and was blessed with the love of wife and child; then one day, when he chanced to look on sickness and death, he became conscious of the wretchedness of human existence, turned his back upon the kingship and the sweet home life, joined himself to the saintly sages of the land, and learned their prescription for a victorious and tranquil life. The prescription which they gave was to make his home in a cave, to procure the barest necessaries of life by begging, to fast to the verge of starvation, and to afflict the body with additional tortures. In the mediæval period of the Christian church, the same conception asserted itself. In the biography of Bernard of Clairvaux we learn incidentally that many men who had within their grasp all that the world could offer of wealth, fame, influence, and human love, turned their backs upon the world, lived as hermits and mendicants, fasted painfully, and even gashed and mutilated their bodies. There has always been a grain of sense even in the wildest extravagances of enthusiasm, and there was a substratum of reason in the ascetic mode of life. It rested on the just observation that there is a keen satisfaction in self-denial which is not yielded by self-indulgence, in particular that the source of a great deal of the worst of human misery is due to the rebellion of the body, and that nothing is more needful than to make sure that what was intended for a slave has not gained the upper hand. But as experience proved that many who were most in earnest in this way of life were not even then at peace, and as moreover common sense effectively protested that there is ample scope for self-denial in labours which are useful to the world, without having recourse to self-inflicted torments which are of no benefit to society, the remedy fell into discredit in Europe with the Protestant Reformation. In Asia it was thrown over by the Buddhists, who were told by their master that, after trial, he had found it a failure, and who advised them rather to seek rest by ceasing from sin, by getting virtue, and by cleansing the heart.

III.

THE STOIC ATTITUDE.

Mention may be made next of the prescription of the Stoics. At the beginning of our era there were many men of great moral earnestness, Greeks and Romans, who claimed to possess in a signal degree the blessing of serenity of mind, especially under the strokes of adversity. How did they teach men to attain to it? We open the pages of Epictetus, and we find the ideas expounded in convenient compass. The things which happen in our life, he says, are of two kinds: those which are due to our own voluntary action, and those which are governed, in whole or in part, by forces that are beyond our control. The goods of life, similarly, are of two kinds: those which, because they are in our power, we can be sure of getting, and those which, being outside our control, we cannot be sure of getting or retaining. The general prescription is that we should limit our desires—confining them to those things which are within our power, and leaving out of account those things which depend upon others. We are not indeed to despise the providential blessings, but to behave in regard to them as one does at a feast—help oneself from a dish when it comes round to us in our turn, but not clamour for it, or call out for it when it has travelled farther round the table. The wise man will not grieve at being poorly furnished in body or mind, or at the coming of sickness and misfortune, because these things were arranged for him; and if he be bereft of a wife or child, he will reflect that this, too, was appointed by a power which he does not control, and also that it should be easy to bear the ills that appertain to the common lot of man. From this general attitude we may certainly learn some practical wisdom. We do well to remember the parable of the feast, and to behave as decently in the struggle for the good things of this world, as we should behave at a dinner-party among our friends. It is also useful to distinguish between the things which are, and those which are not, in our own power, and to cultivate the spirit of uncomplaining submission to the inevitable and irreversible dispensations of Providence. But it is not easy to endure as the Stoic recommended without having access to richer sources of comfort than were supplied by his general view of the universe. He knew only of an unbending and pitiless fate, and such a conception more readily moves us to rebellion than to reverent submission. The human heart in its anguish asks, not for moralisings, but for promises of God.

IV.

CHRIST'S GIFT OF REST.

It was, then, a much-discussed as well as an ancient and widespread malady which Christ promised to cure when He said, "Come unto me all ye that labour and are heavy-laden, and I will give you rest." In His proposed treatment there was a combination of remedies old and new. But even the old appear in a new setting, and with new elements of healing and consolation.

1. There is a strain of the teaching of Jesus which does not contain much more than the advice of the Stoic sages to cut down the demands of the self. The great text in which Christ promises rest, when read along with its context, suggests that the reason why so many are restless is that they do not possess the meekness and lowliness which they could learn from His own example. Their mistake is that they think so much of self, make so much of self, and claim so much for self—especially in the gratification of their pride or vanity—that they are foredoomed to discontent, inasmuch as the world will certainly refuse them many things which they demand, and especially will find many occasions to thwart their ambitious desires and wound their self-esteem. If,

therefore, they could get rid of this spirit by becoming Christlike, their unhappiness would be destroyed, at least in large part, by cutting it away at the root. This is wise teaching, as is convincingly expounded in one of Robertson's memorable sermons, but it is also true—even though the example of Christ has made the counsel 'somewhat easier to follow—that if this were the whole of Christ's prescription we should not be much further advanced than the disciples of the classical sages who were told that the height of wisdom was to moderate their desires in accordance with the best examples of virtuous living.

2. The old and the new also blend, though with a much larger element of the new, in the teaching of our Lord that the chief source of man's unrest is his general sinful condition, and that the secret of rest is deliverance from sin. The Christian account of man's condition is that he is deeply polluted and grievously enslaved by sin, and further that as a consequence the soul lives a turbulent and miserable life. This is incontestably true. Sin is not sustenance for the soul: it is like the husks with which the prodigal, in default of nourishing food, was fain to fill his belly. It is only in God, and in doing the will of God, that the soul finds true rest, and much of human striving is at bottom an attempt to find partial substitutes for God. This would appear to be the ultimate explanation of the craving for stimulants of various kinds, physical or mental; they at least give a temporary feeling that the soul

has found more abundant life and tasted of heaven. It cannot, however, be said that it was a wholly new discovery that sin is the seat of the evil. It had been proclaimed or implied by prophets or psalmists. The way pointed out by Buddha, as has been said, was to find rest by "ceasing from sin." The really new element in the gospel of Christ is its announcement of the way of deliverance from sin. It is a gospel of salvation from the guilt of sin by its wonderful message of free forgiving grace on the ground of the sacrifice once offered of a perfect obedience. It is a gospel of salvation from the power of sin through the baptism of fire which is received in the gift of the Holy Ghost. Its sovereign gift is the infusion of the very life of God into the souls of those who believe with a childlike trust in the economy of grace made known in Jesus Christ.

3. It is a great part of Christ's gift of peace that He enables us to believe in God as the Father in heaven. Buddha preached peace by deliverance from sin, and made some way in teaching men to eradicate their selfish desires, but the soul cannot have true peace if his word was the last word on our little life— " As ye have no Father in heaven to take care of you, see that ye love one another." For those who do not find God in it, the world has no doubt many glories, as it has many privileges and adventures, but it is also a thing of terror. The menacing and destroying forces of time have us at their mercy. We are condemned to the gradual forfeiture of most things

that we value, and in the last resort we are seemingly doomed to extinction. It makes a difference which is almost immeasurable to our outlook on this universe, if we believe in the God whom Christ revealed as the Father, the God who knows each of us, loves and pities us, and who possesses the infinite power and the infinite wisdom which ensure that He will make His loving purposes effective, and that all the hostile powers of earth and time are unable to do any real and deadly hurt either to His cause or to His children. It is because we believe in this God that we can venture more than the Stoic, that we can do more than suffer and be strong. We can contemplate untoward events and even calamities with the persuasion that we do wisely to be tranquil, since love reigns at the heart of things, and we can trust the God of grace, and even the God of Providence, to do all things well, and nothing but what is well.

4. Lastly, there is a deeper and more mystical side. Peace takes possession of the mind in two ways. Sometimes it enters in the wake of ideas, as the result of learning some new or important fact or adopting a fresh conviction. Sometimes also it penetrates the soul in a way of which we cannot easily give a rational explanation. It is a common experience that there are persons the mere contact with whom is restful; their spirit seems to mingle with our spirit and transmit to it some of its own repose. It is a distinctive Christian experience that

a similar peace enters the soul in conscious union and communion with the risen and glorified Christ. He Himself spoke of it in words which implied that His peace was, not so much the result of believing certain facts, and accepting certain doctrines, as the result of the contact of the receptive soul with His own greater personality and His own abounding life. There is an abiding in Him which is the condition of the benediction, "My peace I give unto you."

Every one who is more than a seeming Christian derives from one or other of those sources a certain rest of soul. Even those who are only leavened rather than converted get some benefit from Christ's legacy of rest. The average experience, however, even of those with a real title to the Christian name, is that peace comes and goes, that at least it increases and decreases with their changing moods, and that at the best they only greet afar off the perfect peace for which God is magnified in the hymns of the saints. This being so, it is a somewhat urgent matter that we should try to find out the cause or causes of our disharmony with a view to seeking partial or complete remedies. The sources of the trouble will be found somewhere or other in the ground that we have traversed, and one or two of the more common causes of the disorder may be recalled by way of our practical application.

There can be no doubt that many Christians more than half believe that this world's goods make

16

up the chief good for man. With many others the source of their unsettlement of soul is that they have not decisively put the body in its proper place, and that they do not administer its affairs with wisdom. There are many people in the state of health which is not so serious as to make them seek medical treatment, while yet it is bad enough to afflict them with frequent moods of anxiety, irritation, and depression; and nothing is more important than to find out if their way of living is in any way responsible, and if so to take the body firmly in hand, and insist that it shall become the loyal yoke-fellow and helpmeet of the spirit. Sometimes a candid examination will reveal a worse evil—a habit which must be confessed to be a sinful indulgence, or a neglected duty which avenges itself through an accusing conscience. In the interests of inward peace there can be only one remedy for such a case—to cast from us the evil habit, to take up heartily the omitted task. To many of us a conscientious self-scrutiny will reveal that we are too self-conscious and too self-centred, and a cure has to be sought in some fresh and commanding interest that will take us decisively out of ourselves. Many find a cure by throwing themselves energetically into some form of philanthropic work, when they discover that there is a luxury of doing good which increases rather than palls through repeated gratification. It would be all the better for society, as well as better for those who tried it, if it were commoner for those whose lives are somewhat empty of human love to make the experiment of making some family or individual a peculiar charge. With others the root of their spiritual trouble is that though they may have the essentials of a saving faith, they do not sufficiently trust God as the Power who besets them behind and before, disposes events according to His wise and loving will, and is ever seeking to make all things work together for their good. Finally, it may very well be the case that, even though we have the needed receptivity, we have lacked the faith to claim the deeper experiences of our religion. We may have tarried in the forecourt when there was an invitation for us to enter the Holy of Holies. We have not, perhaps, actually believed in the reality of the mystical relationship which is the heart of our Christian religion—in the spiritual heaven which the Saviour promised when He said that He, and with Him the Father, would make their abode in the hearts which were made ready to receive them by faith and love. With less than this we may be in a state of grace, and may even struggle on passably with a modicum of peace through life's labours and trials; but towards the mystical union with God we must aspire if the peace which passeth understanding is to begin to keep our hearts and minds. Amen.

XVII.

RETROSPECT AND PROSPECT.

"One day which shall be known to the Lord : not day, nor night : but it shall come to pass, that at evening time it shall be light."—ZECHARIAH xiv. 7.

ON the last day of 1916 we look back on the chequered experiences of nearly two and a half years of the great war. We have had our disappointments and our trials, but when we consider the general trend of events, and the central features of the situation, we may feel thankful to God and possess our souls in quietness and confidence.

I.

THE COURSE OF EVENTS.

During the first eighteen months of the war our enemies had a series of successes which only fell short of a victorious decision. In the first rush on Paris they drove the French and British armies before them ; and although they met with an ominous check on the Marne, which was repeated in the first battle of Ypres, they remained in possession of Belgium, and of rich districts of Northern France. At the same time they very effectively stopped the Russian invasion of Prussian territory. In 1915 they had again reason to ring the bells in Berlin and Vienna, when the Russian hosts, instead of sweeping on through Silesia to Berlin, were shattered by the German artillery. They were strong enough, while holding back France and Britain with the left hand, to deal a blow with the right arm which drove the Russians far beyond the Vistula, and gave them Poland as their spoil. But in 1916 their campaigns have shown a heavy balance of failure. They made four attempts to repeat their overwhelming stroke, and three of the attempts signally failed. From February to June they concentrated their military skill and their Teutonic fury in the onslaught on Verdun, and to-day they have recoiled almost to the point from which they set out, and tens of thousands of their dead lie buried on ground which has again been wrested from them by the French. The Austrians co-operated by a similar assault on the Italian lines, and after an initial success they were flung back beyond their own frontier. The Turks did their allotted part by a descent on Egypt, and they have been routed and chased back to the borders of Palestine. The fourth project was to punish Rumania for her adhesion to the cause of the Allies, and at the same time to capture her stores of corn and oil, and this plan has been successfully carried

out, at least on the military side. But when we
consider the situation as a whole, we may well think
that the Rumanian expedition was in a way an
evidence of weakness. It may be remembered that
when Ivanhoe entered the lists at the tournament of
Ashby-de-la-Zouche, a sympathetic onlooker advised
him to challenge, not the accomplished Templar, or
the redoubtable Front-de-Bœuf, but the Knight of St.
John. "He has the least sure seat," he cried; "he
is your cheapest bargain." It is quite certain that
Germany, if she had had the power, would have
struck her annihilating blow at France or Russia, and
still more at Britain; and when, instead of attempting
anything so considerable, she flung a reserve army
against the ill-equipped Rumanians, we may reasonably think the explanation was that this was the
only quarter in which she could hope to snatch the
victory which was needed to revive the flagging
energies and the fading hopes of the people.

To these attempts has to be added the renewal of
the special campaign against Great Britain by air and
sea. The aerial monsters, it was believed, would
strike consternation into our heart, and the monsters
of the deep would cut off our daily bread. And it
would be vain to deny that we have been injured
as well as exasperated by the novel forms of assault.
It was a shock to our comfortable sense of insular
security when a giant airship sailed over an English
city, and rained destruction on defenceless inhabitants of the suburb and the tenement. It was also

painful to realise that, under the new conditions of warfare, there were limitations to our Navy's powers —that a German cruiser could make a furtive raid and bombard an English seaport, and still worse, that hundreds of our merchantmen, trawlers, and liners could be sent by torpedoes to the bottom of the sea. But the results of these activities have fallen far short of the expectations. The general effect of the air raids has been to arouse indignation rather than fear: we have accepted them as an addition to the dangers and the ills of human life, which for destructiveness may rank with fires and railway accidents, and which should not—unless we are old or nervous—do much more to affect our tranquillity than these standing dangers to limb and life. The submarine warfare has more seriously injured us, but even in this case the wound has only been a flesh-wound, which instead of depressing and weakening us has rather steeled the will and focussed the strength. The highest hopes were reposed in the weapon of the submarine. It was to wear down our Navy by a process of attrition, and it was to establish on the high seas a reign of terror, which would cut off from our ports the ships that carry to us so large a store of the materials of our industry and of the necessaries of life. The attempt on the Navy has miscarried: we have reason to believe that it is stronger, both absolutely and relatively, than at the commencement of the war. The merchant service has suffered, but in the course of the year the German submarine service had also suffered so heavily that for a season it took a comparative rest because of its weakness, and claimed credit for its inaction as a concession to the American conscience. And although it is serious news that the under-sea campaign is to be renewed on a larger scale, and by the most ruthless methods, we may take heart to believe that, as the task of our Navy is a species of sea-fishing, it will become ever more expert in the exercise of its craft. The German navy is a formidable force. It ventured out at length into the open, and fought the battle of Jutland; and though sorely battered and weakened, it returned to its secure haven, and covered its retreat with boasts which contained a disagreeable admixture of fact with fiction. It gained so much credit in the great naval battle that one is surprised that the Germans should have done their best to make it an object of ridicule by pretending that it has the command of the North Sea, and asking their people to believe this because of an occasional raid in which shells are thrown on a coast-town, or a destroyer steals home with a prize. Every schoolboy is acquainted with a mischievous agility which is different from strength, and it is difficult to believe that the mind of the German people has not grasped the distinction. We at least may feel confident that as before, and even more than before, our Navy is, under God, the sure shield of these islands, and that its command of the seas is the omen of complete victory.

It is significant of the changed situation that in

1916 the story of the war was no longer exclusively the story of German successes or failures.   The initiative, which they look on as the symbol of the winning cause, passed in great measure to the Allies.   The Russians resumed their campaign with a renewed strength which shook the whole Austrian position; and the French and the Italians, after beating off their assailants, proceeded to a vigorous counter-offensive.   But the outstanding event of the year was the advent of Great Britain with the numbers and the equipment of a first-class military power. We had thrown our whole strength into the preparations—we had trained at least 4,000,000 of the flower of our manhood for war service, directed the plant and the skill of our workshops to the provision of military supplies, and put in pledge for the outlays the whole of the national fortune.   On July 1st, in concert with the French, our Army struck at the German front on the Somme, and pierced their lines in a section of some half-dozen miles.   Our soldiers pressed on, supported by terrific artillery fire, through the widening breach, and fought long-drawn and desperate battles for the possession of a ruined village or a wood-clad height; and although there were checks and pauses, and the expected toll of loss had to be paid to the full, the enemy was hurled from many a stronghold which had been deemed impregnable, and the advance continued in an unresting and tenacious fashion that bore a welcome resemblance to the tightening grasp of fate.   When it is considered

that during these months the British and French
divisions fought on the Somme against one-half of the
German army, that positions which the Germans were
ordered to hold at all costs were wrested from them,
and that they left nearly 80,000 prisoners in the
hands of the Allies, we may trustfully accept the report of our commander-in-chief that the longest and
bloodiest battle in history terminated in our favour,
and still more confidently may we believe that our
nation has created and equipped a force that will have
a decisive influence on the issue of the war.

II.

THE ARM OF THE LORD.

Has the arm of the Lord been revealed in the
events of the war? It was of evil omen for the Scots
before the battle of Pinkie, John Knox observes, that
the leaders said, "We have hands enough," and "no
word of God." It is certain, if we may follow the
Old Testament prophets, that God has at least been
challenged to "make bare his holy arm," for the
deepest conviction of the prophets was that God is
the guardian of the moral order of the world. In
particular we may note these forms of national wickedness which they believed that God must restrain and
punish.

1. It was the belief of the prophets that God is
against a nation which wantonly lets loose the horrors

of war upon the earth. "He hath scattered the peoples," says the Psalmist, "that delight in war" (lxviii. 30). Martin Luther was fond of quoting this text, and he added that, so far as his knowledge went, God had never failed to call the aggressor to a reckoning. But Luther's warning fell on deaf ears. There is one European people which, for generations, has been taught to glorify war, and which has been prepared for it with a degree of forethought, thoroughness, and inventiveness which must be the envy of the Powers of Darkness.

2. It was also a principle of the prophets that national pride invites the chastening strokes of Heaven. This is a leading idea of the song called the Magnificat: "He hath scattered the proud in the imagination of their hearts." Isaiah in particular declared the wrath of God against human insolence. It was the sin which had made Babylon an offence to God as well as the scourge of mankind.

"Thou hast said in thine heart, I will ascend into heaven, I will exalt my throne above the stars of God.

"I will ascend above the heights of the clouds; I will be like the Most High." And the punishment will fit the transgression.

"How art thou fallen from heaven, O Lucifer, son of the morning! how art thou cut down to the ground, which didst weaken the nations!

"They that see thee shall narrowly look upon thee, and consider thee, saying, Is this the man that made the earth to tremble, that did shake kingdoms;

"That made the world as a wilderness, and destroyed the cities thereof?" (xiv. 12 ff.).

Every nation is to be allowed self-respect, and there is a margin of vanity which is venial, but there is one gifted people which in recent times developed a morbid self-consciousness and an arrogance which would not have been justified if it had been a compendium of all the most famous nations of history.

3. The chiefest maxim of the prophets is that God is moved to punish a nation for flagrant acts of injustice and inhumanity. Amos gives a list of acts which provoked God to cast down princes, and send fire upon their cities (i. 3 ff.). Damascus threshed Gilead with threshing instruments of iron. The Philistines sent some of the Israelites into slavery: The Phœnicians broke a treaty. The children of Ammon massacred the women with their babes that they might enlarge their border. With one exception the particulars in Amos's list are somewhat closely paralleled by the doings of Germany in the present war, and they have even had some original additions; while the example of Ammon has been somewhat closely followed by Turkey in the renewal of her attempt to solve her Armenian problem by the process of extermination. We must admit that the moral standard is inevitably lowered in the essentially unethical conditions of war, and we can make allowances for the passions when a population is suffering some of the privations of a beleaguered fortress; but it

does not seem open to doubt that Germany's conduct of the war has fallen below the irreducible minimum demanded by modern decency and humanity.

Is there any evidence that the God of history has responded to the challenge of those who have thus roughly defied the moral order? Our fore-fathers were wont to look through the eyes of the Old Testament prophets, and would have reminded us that the God of Providence, even when He does not wholly overthrow the forces of evil, at least impedes their operations and frustrates their designs. And even to some who are not predisposed to religious thinking, it has seemed that in this war the German plans have come into collision with the impediments of Providence. Germany was foiled in her main purpose when she had very excellent grounds for expecting that with her available numbers, her equipment of guns and material, her carefully thought-out plans, her swiftness of movement, her concentrated blows, and the unreadiness of her enemies, she would crash through all defences in a brief campaign. Had she been victorious in the battle of the Marne, it would probably have been decisive; and when we have heard all that has been told of the circumstances of that battle, we may well feel that we can only explain the event on the supposition that Providence on that day helped the weaker things to confound those which were mightier.

Still more impressively, perhaps, have the events of the war confirmed the maxim of the prophets that it is the way of God to humble the pride of man. We ourselves have been touched in the article of our pride. We undertook to deal with Turkey, and we have not had all the best of the encounter. If we had an idol it was our Fleet, and we have been made to chafe under the limitations of its powers. But if we have been made uncomfortable, Germany has been sore stricken by the irony of Heaven. In two things she felt more pride than is permitted to mortals—her army and her intellect—and through both her pride has undergone a mortification that has the aspect of an ironical judgment. On the route which she had chosen for a triumphal procession into France her path is barred by the amateur armies of Britain. Her vaunted intelligence so failed her that she is proved to have miscalculated in most of the expectations which encouraged her to begin the war, and she has blundered into ways which were not only wicked but stupid, and have left her without one disinterested friend. The God of the prophets still does things in the world.

III.

A TIME FOR WAR AND A TIME FOR PEACE.

The time for peace has not yet come. Recently the Central Powers made known their willingness to enter on negotiations. The President of the United States followed with a request which had the appearance of being sensible—that the belligerent powers should descend from generalities, and state the concrete proposals which they would regard as yielding a tolerable settlement. The same attitude is credited to the Pope; and although the policy of the Vatican is usually on a quite mundane level, I can believe that the Pope feels it his duty, as a Christian man, to try and put an immediate stop to the appalling havoc and bloodshed. But there are grave objections to the course which seems so obvious to Mr. Wilson and to the Pope. It seems rather hopeless to look for a useful discussion of terms so long as each combatant maintains that he is the victor and the other the vanquished. Nor is it at all evident that those who hold Christian principles ought to work for the earliest possible peace. The Allies believe themselves to be, not parties to a sordid dispute, but sufferers by a criminal enterprise. The motive was predatory, the act was premeditated, the moment was carefully chosen, and the methods subsequently employed have been of the kind which is expected of a private malefactor when he is caught in the toils. It is often advisable to compromise a civil suit, but in a criminal case it is the duty of a good citizen to help to bring an offender to justice, so that society may be protected against a repetition of the injury. And the very natural and proper position of the Allies is, that they do not propose to compound a felony.

IV.

THE OUTLOOK.

It is to be expected, unless some unforeseen developments should take place, that the war will go on at least until the late autumn of 1917. It will obviously take months before full effect is given to our reserves of power. The year will mark the climax, not only of our efforts, but of our sacrifices. The end will not be reached without repetitions of the struggle which we have breathlessly watched on the Somme, and without a corresponding toll of the best and bravest of our race. It will not be reached without its being brought home to every family that, having accepted such a war, we must be prepared to pay the price in loss of goods, in privations of body, and in anguish of soul. But we may also expect that the spirit of our people will stand the strain. It commits many sins in ignorance, but it does not lie in its nature to be wilfully weak or cowardly. It was never its way to look back when it had put its hand to the plough. Nothing is more striking in the period through which we are passing than the fact that our public men do not make speeches exhorting us to be strong and endure to the end: they take for granted that that is our intention. Having been assured that the goal is attainable, our people can be depended on, from instinct as well as from principle, to proceed to finish the rough, grim work of justice which, in the August of 1914, it accepted as its appointed task.

Even now Germany has been baffled; and we hope that within another year she will have been mastered. I live in the faith that the world is subject to a divine government which has purposed to restrain her violence and confound her plots. From the purely human point of view we have very solid grounds of confidence. The increasing pressure of the greatly superior resources of the Allies in men, materials, and money must slowly wear down the Teutonic strength; and apart from any private impression of the state of affairs, we can safely infer from the nature of the reply of the Allies to the recent suggestion of peace, that those whose business it is to know the facts are assured of our ability to convert our advantages into an acknowledged victory. Had peace been concluded after the campaigns of 1916, the most we could have expected was the restoration of the general situation as it existed before the war—with the serious difference that we should have found ourselves half crushed by the burden of our recent losses, and yet doomed to make costly preparations against fresh intrigues and schemes of conquest. What we hope for as the reward of another year's labours and sacrifices is that they will shatter Germany's dream of domination in Europe, and break her power to strive for it; more than this, that they will decide that no further attempt is to be made henceforth to use Europe as a theatre of

17

military adventure, and that there will be a new settlement which will be based generally on the principle that each nationality is entitled to security and liberty, and that it is the duty of the European family as a whole to uphold the rights of each member of the circle.

It is quite likely that some of the most important consequences of the great war will be very different from anything that was intended by the authors, or even by others of the actors in the drama. There will be new illustrations of the irony of God —that striking principle of the providential government which is compounded of the divine wisdom and retributive justice, and has affinity with what we know as humour in man. It will be a striking example of the principle if the German militarism which took over the military ambitions of Alexander the Great and of Napoleon should prove, as we hope, to have paved the way for the reign of peace among a free United States of Europe. It would be another event of the same sort, certainly undesigned in the ambitions either of Germany or of Russia, if, as a consequence of the clash of the Empires, Poland was restored to her former place among the European nations. It may also happen that the Kaiser, who sowed the wind of foreign war, will reap the whirlwind of domestic revolution, and that the greatest result of his reign for Germany will be, that he will be found to have undermined the throne of the Hohenzollerns and paved the way for the triumph of German democracy. It would also be one of the unexpected effects of history, if it should prove that the chief lesson which the allied nations had learned in frustrating the Teutonic conspiracy was the duty of setting their own houses in order.

If the sacrifices of this war are to be justified by results, measures will be taken to ensure that it will be the last, at least the last of the same magnitude. As man is a rational and moral being, he is bound eventually to organise a league of nations which will dispose of international disputes by the method of inquiry and trial, and use the collective power to enforce the verdicts. Probably there was a time when people said that, human nature being what it was, individuals would never agree to defer to a judge and to be controlled by a policeman; and those who say the same thing to-day about nations will doubtless also be confuted by the event. The conception of the nations as a family, which should devise a moral and peaceable way of settling its quarrels, is an ideal which ought to command the whole-hearted allegiance of the civilised nations, and especially of the Christian Church. And it is in the light of this ideal that we must think of the future of Germany, if she should emerge from this war broken and chastened, and offering reparation and amendment. It would be quite inconsistent with our general conception of the future to think of her as the subject of a prolonged process of boycotting, or going about with a ticket-of-leave. The generation which has wrought the present iniquity on the earth will pass away, and those who follow will rightly claim to be treated on their own merits. Without the German people the European family circle would be very incomplete, and the variety of the family life would be seriously reduced. Some of us, accordingly, who think nothing is more Christian at the present stage than the relentless prosecution of the war, will think it a most urgent Christian duty, when justice has been done, to labour for a reconciliation. It is inconceivable that we should hold the principle of human brotherhood subject to the exclusion of the Germans from its operation. It may be added that, when a repentant Germany falls in with the ideal of a League of Peace, she may be expected to become one of the most zealous and efficient of the contributors to the measures that may be occasionally necessary in the way of policing the world.

And what of the result for the British Empire and for the homeland? It has long been assured that the British Empire is safe in this crisis. It was a saying of Treitschke that nothing was so remarkable about it as its persistent good fortune, and he could adduce nothing so remarkable from its history as the events of the last three years. We might have been overwhelmed in our unpreparedness; and as a fact we were practically given two years' notice in which to teach our men the use of the soldier's tools, and to produce the instruments and the munitions of war. The Empire might have fallen in pieces in the shock of such a conflict, and the shock has only served to increase the stability of the fabric and to bind the parts more closely together.   In the light of those facts we may well have faith to believe that our Empire roughly stands for ideals—such as order, justice, and humanity—which are those of the Kingdom of God, and that the God of Providence finds in it a serviceable instrument for the furtherance of His general purpose with mankind.   From the human point of view, it may at least be said that our Empire, in so far as it is a confederation of self-governing peoples united by devotion to a greater whole, is a unique organisation which has deserved to live, and which is not only likely to be imitated by other groups of peoples, but may also prove a model to suggest general lines of the organisation of the human race in its entirety.   Upon our domestic conditions the effects of the war will doubtless be great and far-reaching.   Our difficulties and our failures were largely due to habits which had been moulded by the excessive respect for private rights and liberties, which is concisely described as individualism ; during the war we have become habituated to subordinate practically everything to the safety and well-being of the commonwealth ; and it seems certain that we shall continue to grapple in the same spirit with those permanent ills of society which, after all, only differ in degree from the calamities of war.

If analogy may be trusted, the unexampled conflict should bring a harvest of spiritual results.   The great struggles of the past have often been followed by a remarkable stimulation of the higher life of humanity, and by the subsequent appearance of a generation of great men. We are probably justified in looking forward to a similar compensation and consolation. We already see the beginnings of a moral conversion. The mark of the children of the new age will surely be that self will be less central in their thinking than it was in ours. We may also confidently look forward to a fresh out-pouring of the Holy Spirit. It is manifestly the settled purpose of God in the spiritual realm, no less than in the natural, to continue to send showers to water the earth, and to make it bring forth its fruits. History encourages us to hope that, after a convulsion like the present, the Spirit will return in power to bind up the wounds of humanity, and to renew its faith and its courage. God, it is true, acts in un-expected ways; and He may disappoint some by not exactly repeating the forms and the message of earlier Pentecosts. But the Spirit will at least con-tinue to testify of Christ, and show the things of Christ. And we may rest assured that sooner or later there will be given a new experience, and a new certainty of God, so that men will say, " I have heard of thee by the hearing of the ear, but now mine eye seeth thee." The Lord hasten it in our time. Amen.

Printed by MORRISON & GIBB LIMITED, Edinburgh

HISTORY OF CHRISTIAN MISSIONS

By Canon CHARLES HENRY ROBINSON, D.D.

Editorial Secretary of the S.P.G. in Foreign Parts

'We have here a work of the highest importance and authority on a subject commended by Christ Himself to the lasting interest and aspirations of Christians. It is the work of an expert ; as regards history and statistics it says the last word on Missions up to the present date. . . . It is quite impossible to indicate adequately the worth and profound interest of the work.'—*Guardian*.

Price 9/- net

THE LATIN CHURCH IN THE MIDDLE AGES

By ANDRÉ LAGARDE

'There are many good histories of the mediæval Church, English, French, and German, and this is certainly one of the very best. It does not deal, as the temptation is to do, simply with picturesque incidents or personages (how strange a saying it was of Bishop Creighton's, that the Middle Ages lacked "picturesque and emancipated individuals") ; or with opposing principles. It gives us an account of the Pontifical exchequer, it unfolds the methods of Episcopal elections, it tells of heresies and their suppression, of the studies of the clergy and of ecclesiastical writers. It is difficult to say which is the most interesting part of a singularly well-written and well-arranged book.'—*Guardian*.

Price 10/6 net

'SUB CORONA'

Sermons preached in the Chapel of King's College, Aberdeen

By Principals Sir GEORGE ADAM SMITH, J. IVERACH, J. DENNEY, ALEX. STEWART ; Professors D. S. CAIRNS, J. COOPER, W. A. CURTIS, J. GILROY, D. M. KAY, A. R. MACEWEN, J. E. MCFADYEN, H. R. MACKINTOSH, G. MILLIGAN, T. NICOL, W. P. PATERSON, H. M. B. REID, J. A. SELBIE, J. STALKER, H. COWAN ; The Bishop of ABERDEEN and ORKNEY.

Edited by Prof. H. COWAN and Dr. J. HASTINGS

'The sermons cover a wide range, but all are practical and evangelical, simple in style, yet full of thought and ripe wisdom. It is a book that preachers will be eager to study, and from which they will learn much.'

London Quarterly Review.

In the 'Scholar as Preacher' Series, price 4/6 net

THE MYTHICAL INTERPRETA-TION OF THE GOSPELS

By THOMAS J. THORBURN, D.D., LL.D.

'All these men (Prof. DREWS, Prof. W. B. SMITH, Dr. JENSEN, Mr. J. M. ROBERTSON, &c.) have given themselves to the elaboration of the proof that Christ and the Gospels are a product of a myth-making tendency inveterate in the human race. . . . Dr. Thorburn has no mercy. He has made so special a study of the subject that nothing escapes him. He brings out their contradictions and incredible blunders with the calmness and precision of a trained detective.'—*Expository Times.*

Price 7/6 net

PRAYER

By JAMES HASTINGS, D.D.

The first of a short series of Volumes on

THE GREAT CHRISTIAN DOCTRINES

'Nothing could have been more appropriate than this volume on "Prayer" during a world-crisis like the present. All the elements of prayer—adoration, confession, petition, intercession, thanksgiving—are treated in turn, while the nature of prayer, together with scientific and philosophic objections, is amply considered. Further, there are chapters on encouragements, perplexities, answers, times, and manner of prayer. . . . As a text-book for Christian preachers, teachers, and workers, the book will prove of the utmost service.'

London Quarterly Review.

Price 6/- net

THE IDEALS OF THE PROPHETS

By Prof. S. R. DRIVER, D.D.

Edited by CANON G. A. COOKE, D.D. With a Bibliography of Dr Driver's published writings

'The treatment is throughout characterised by the exact scholarship and sobriety of judgment which have for many years led students to regard the preacher as the most reliable of English critics of the modern school in the field of Old Testament research.'—*Christian World.*

Price 3/6 net

Lightning Source UK Ltd.
Milton Keynes UK
UKHW020334221118
332685UK00006B/702/P

9 780483 227521